About the author

Tony was born in Nottingham in 1952. In his twenties the seeds were sown for his love affair with Greece, during a holiday on the island of Skiathos. Since then he has visited many of the islands of the Ionian and Aegean seas, as well as the mainland of Greece.

His heart though lies on the small-unspoilt islands of the Aegean. When in 2006 he had the opportunity of semi-retiring from his business consultancy, he and his partner Carol chose Thassos as their base as UK ex-pats, selecting to live on the outskirts of Thassos Town, known locally as Limenas.

As an author of business books, Tony had been aware after his many years travelling within Greece that what was lacking for the holidaymaker and general traveller was a 'no holds barred' guide to the islands, with *all* the information that is required to have an exciting, informative and safe vacation brought together in one easy to read book.

And so, in 2006 he decided to write this first book on the island of Thassos. Since then Tony has written further guide books on the islands of Kos and Santorini. He hopes that in the years to come, his continuing travels will allow him to write guides for the other Greek islands that he loves.

Opposite: Thassian silver Trihemiobol coin, with the ithyphallic figure of Silenus, bearded with a horses tail, kneeling holding a Kantharos, 390 - 350 B.C.

A-Z Guide to

Thassos

including Kavala and Philippi

Tony Oswin

Contents:
The island, its history, what to see, where to go, eating out, the best beaches, travel information and a host of tips and hints for the holidaymaker and traveller.

2008 edition

Published 2007 by Lulu publishing
www.lulu.com/uk
7th edition

ISBN: 978-1-84728-253-8

Typeset in Arial 9/10/12/14/16/20/48

To my partner Carol....for all her loving support

Foreword

I have been travelling to Greece for over thirty years and during that time I have fallen in love with the country, its people and most of all the Greek approach to life.

However, I realised many years ago, that one thing that was missing for the holidaymaker and visitor to the Greek islands, was a comprehensive publication written by someone who lives there, with *all* the necessary information and 'insider' knowledge, brought together in one easy to read book. Too many times, I have returned home from a visit to Greece, only to talk to someone who has advised me of something I should have done or seen, that I had been unaware of.

Hence this book, I hope you find it helpful and informative, not only during your stay, but in the planning stage back in the UK (or wherever you live).

Due to the wonders of modern publishing, the information within this book will be updated on a regular basis and I would appreciate the readers' feedback by email to help in the revision and improvement of the information contained herein. Through this, I aim to keep the book fresh, comprehensive and accurate.

For the latest information and news obtained mid-revision, you will find a 'Newsflash' page on the website detailed below.

I hope you have a wonderful visit to Thassos. See you on the beach!

email: info@a-to-z-guide.co.uk

To view the other books in the 'A to Z series' visit

www.a-to-z-guide.co.uk

Contents

Thassos

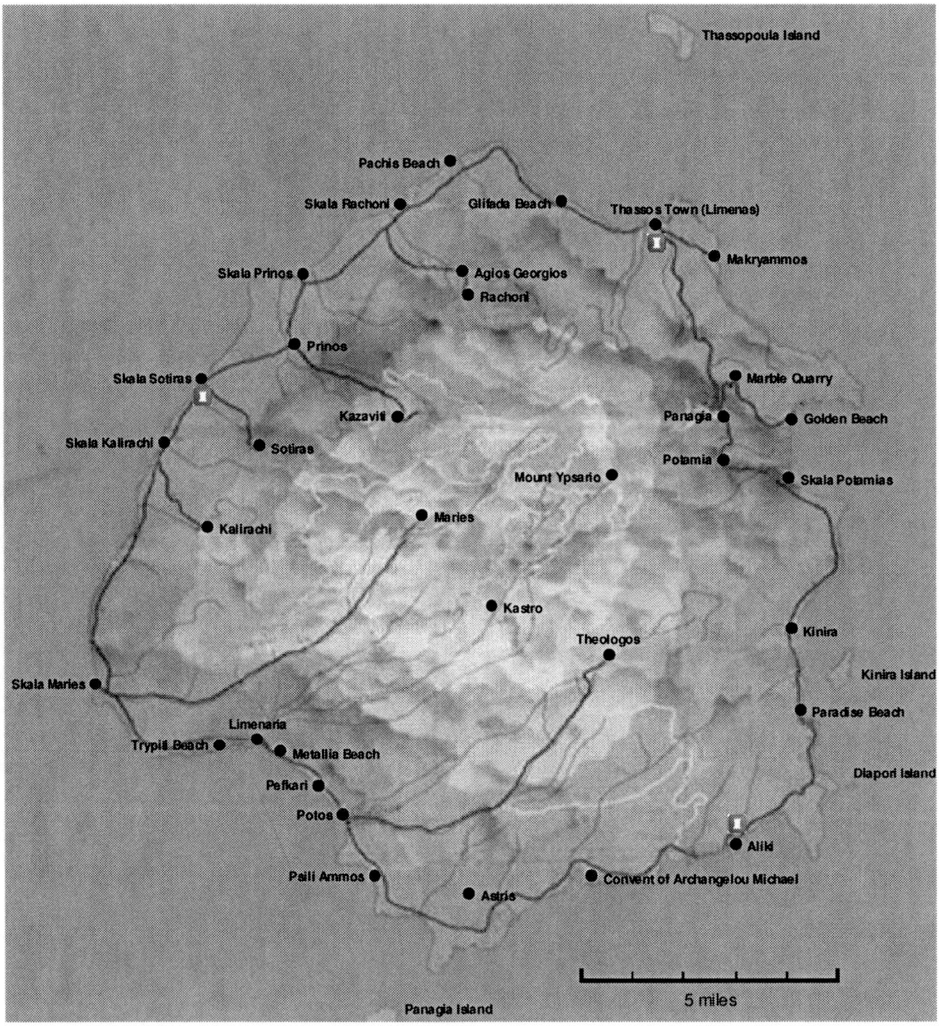

Archaeological sites

'The jewel of the Aegean'

Thassos or **Thasos** (Greek: Θάσος) is an island in the northern Aegean Sea, situated just off the coast of Macedonia and Thrace and opposite Kavala, the largest city and port in northeast Greece.

The highest elevation on Thassos is Mount Ypsario at 1,204 metres. The main agricultural production on the island comprises honey and olive oil and to a lesser extent wine, sheep, goats and fishing. The main industries include tourism, quarrying and timber.

The island's surface area is 393 sq km (25 km by 21 km at its widest points) and has a population of 13,765 (2001 Census). It is one of the provinces of Kavala Region (which includes part of the mainland), comprising, in terms of administration, 1 Municipality (the Municipality of Thassos) and 9 Communities.

A visit to Thassos will confirm that it has much more to offer than just beautiful beaches and turquoise seas. Here you will still find a continuing respect for Greek culture and tradition, which is sadly being lost on many of the other islands, as they become evermore tourist orientated. The Thassians have a rich history, with archaeological sites scattered throughout the island, so you can combine a relaxing beach holiday, with one that includes an interesting delve into ancient history.

Thassos is mountainous, on the eastern and southern coasts this terrain extends all the way down to the sea. In the west, plains stretch from the base of the mountains to the shoreline. Much of the island's surface area is covered with thick forests of pine, fir, oak, chestnut, walnut and plane trees and although the timber is still logged for the shipbuilding and construction industries, the trade has reduced in importance in recent years.

Thassos has an abundance of freshwater springs and is the most fertile island in the Aegean Sea, producing cereals, legumes, fruit, honey and wine. In the coastal areas olives are extensively cultivated. Aromatic plants such as myrtle, oregano, sage, thyme and rosemary perfume the air throughout the summer months.

There is an abundant supply of minerals on the island, with copper in the districts of Astris, Thimonia and Theologos; lead, silver and zinc in Limenaria and iron in the district of Kallirachi. In antiquity the famous Roman writer Pliny noted that the island was also a source of gems such as opals and amethysts.

The marble quarries of Thassos, have since antiquity, supplied the high quality all white marble to the many civilisations of the Mediterranean and beyond. Thassian marble was used in the construction of one of the Byzantine Empire's most magnificent buildings, namely the church of Saint Sophia in Constantinople (Hagia Sophia). Today it is a major export from the island, with the largest marble quarries being in the Vathy and Panagia regions. The former is an impressive site when viewed from the ferry as you arrive or leave the island. It stands out as a large white scar on the mountain to the far left of Thassos town.

With all these qualities, it is not surprising that Thassos has the highest percentage of revisits of holidaymakers of all the Greek islands, with many returning year after year.

However, if you are looking for the 'Ibiza' of Greece, Thassos is not for you.

History

The history of Thassos is one of invasion and subjugation, with consecutive conquerors coveting not only the resources of the island, but also its strategic position. There is certainly evidence that the island was inhabited in the Palaeolithic and Neolithic age ('Old' and 'New' Stone Ages), with the discovery of ochre mines and artefacts in the region of Maries and Neolithic settlements at Kastri, near Theologos and Limenaria. Remains of settlers dating back to the 4th and 3rd millenniums B.C., have been found on the island especially around Skala Sotiras (see page 57) and Kastri. Similar remains have also been found on the shoreline of the facing mainland and throughout the Aegean and Asia Minor, confirming the extensive migration and colonisation of the Aegean people in this period.

Since antiquity, the island has been known by many different names, the earliest reflect the names of the tribes of people who settled, such as the Sedon and Odones from mainland Thrace, others are descriptive names of the island, covered later in the section on 'Mythology'. There is historical mention of the Carians on Thassos, who it is said were allies of Troy and took up arms against the Greeks in the Trojan War. Another tribe the Pelasgoi, are also identified as possible colonists. It has been said that the Phoenicians came to Thassos to exploit the local mines and timber, especially in the area of Kinira in the period 1,600 to 1,500 B.C. The famous Greek historian Herodotus (484 - c.425 B.C.) mentions this in his writings. However, no artefacts that can be attributed to the Phoenicians have yet been found on the island.

Around 680 B.C., Thassos was threatened by Thracian tribes, the islanders turned to their allies on Paros (an island in the southern Aegean) requesting military aid. Telesicles the King of Paros agreed, but consulted the oracle at Delphi first, receiving the following prophecy. "Tell the Parians, Telesicles, that I have ordered you to build upon the Isle of Aeria a great city that will be visible from all around." So Telesicles with his son (or grandson) Archilochos and later with his great general, Glaukos, led forces that successfully defeated the Thracians, settling Parians on the island until it could count a population of more than 60,000 and was known as 'The Athens of the North'. This growth was founded on the rich natural resources of marble, gold, silver and iron as well as its agricultural products especially the highly praised wine.

By the late 6th century B.C., Thassos had grown into a powerful city-state that colonised the facing coast of Macedonia, fortified the island's capital and was renowned as a major naval force in the area. Both Athens and Sparta endeavoured to take Thassos under their influence and they managed to do so by starting wars in turn. It was plain to see that whoever dominated Thassos, would benefit not only from its strategic position, but also from the resources of the island and its mainland colonies. It was at this time that the island experienced a period of extensive development, its people cultivating the art of sculpture, architecture and theatre, many of the elements of which survive to this day. In the field of athletic achievements, Thassos boasts one of the Olympic Champions of antiquity, Theagenis (see page 45).

By the 5th century, Thassos had a population of 150,000; powerful walls surrounded Limenas the island's city, where there was a fortified naval harbour and a commercial harbour (Limenas, means 'The Harbour'), a prytaneum, a market, a theatre and a conservatory (a school of music and the dramatic arts). A prytaneum was the ancient equivalent of today's Town Hall, where government business was administered and official hospitality was extended to distinguished citizens and visitors to the island.

In 477 B.C., the island joined the Delian League (the Delian League, led by Athens, was an association of Greek city-states allied against Persia), but in 465 B.C. they defected from the league, resulting in Athens besieging the island. After two years of siege, the island capitulated and signed a treaty with Athens that imposed severe penalties. These included the confiscation of their naval fleet and the destruction of the city walls.

The decline of Thassos as an independent state began after the Persian Wars of 499 - 448 B.C. (see Greek timeline page 82), after when it fell under the administration of Athens. Sparta though also coveted the island and in 405 invaded and took control, only to have the island ally itself once again with Athens in 375, as a member of the second Athenian League.

In 338 B.C., Thassos was subjugated by the King of Macedonia Philip II, father of Alexander the Great. After the Battle of Cynoscephalae in 197 B.C., the island was 'freed' from Macedonian domination by Rome and became relatively independent. However during the reign of Vespasian (69 - 79 A.D.), Thassos was fully appropriated by Rome as a province of Thrace, under Rome's direct control. In 330 A.D., the Holy Roman Empire's capital moved to Constantinople (Byzantium) and the island became part of the Byzantine Empire.

During the Byzantine period, invasions and piracy were a major problem for the island and from the 7th century A.D., an intensification of raids forced the inhabitants to move from the shoreline and build villages further up the mountains, hence the 'dual villages', one at sea level (Skala) and one further inland.

In the late 1300's, the Byzantines besieged the island, but were unsuccessful in taking it. In 1414 A.D. the Genoese Jacomo Gattilusi seized the island, and his family held it until 1479 when the Turks took the island over. During the Turkish occupation of 1479 to 1770 the Turks deported most of the citizens and the island was left uninhabited. The Russian/Turkish war of 1770 saw the island seized by the Russians, but they departed in 1774 and the island returned to Turkish rule.

In 1813 Thassos was granted by the Turkish Sultan to the Vizier of Egypt, Mehmet Ali, who was the founder of the Basilica Dynasty of Egypt. He was born in Kavala and raised by a family in the village of Rachoni on Thassos (his birthplace and residence is covered in 'Visiting Kavala', page 58). Out of gratitude, Mehmet Ali freed the island from most taxes, however even this act didn't pacify the Thassians. In 1821 they unsuccessfully rebelled against Egyptian rule, led by the chieftain Chadjigeorgis Metaxas from Theologos. After the failure of the revolt, Metaxas left the island, accepting responsibility to prevent reprisals against the population.

In 1902 new taxes sparked further unrest, resulting in the end of the Egyptian administration of the island and the beginning, once again, of the Turkish occupation. In 1912 it was liberated by the Greek navy, a year later becoming officially part of the Greek state.

In 1939 at the beginning of the Second World War, Greece was invaded by Italy. However the Greek army routed the Italians and drove them back to the Albanian mountains. To save face and for strategic reasons, Germany as allies of Italy, diverted forces to aid the Italians and in 1940 the Axis forces defeated the Greek army and occupied the country. The Greeks suffered enormously under the German administration, both through starvation and severe restrictions. Later the Germans handed the administration over to their allies the Bulgarians, who's military and political authorities continued the severe treatment of the local population, until in November 1944 the Axis forces in Greece surrendered.

The Greek civil war (1946 -1949) was the first example of a post-war communist insurgency in Europe. The victory of the anti-communist government forces, led to Greece's membership in NATO and defined the 'Cold War' balance of power in the Aegean.

Mythology

According to one version of the myth, Thassos was the island of the Sirens who possessed women's features, but from the waist down had the form of a bird. One played the lyre, another sang, and another played the flute. Through their enchanting music and deceit, they persuaded passing mariners to linger and when they were at their ease, they consumed them. That is why Thassos was said to be full of the bones of those who had perished. The ancient myths are inconsistent about the number of Sirens, some saying there were two, others three (as above), with some giving more than three names: Aglaope, Leucosia, Parthenope, Pisinoe and Thelxiepia. Whatever the number, it was said that they would impart knowledge and wisdom and enchant every man who heard them.

When the Argonauts (of 'Jason and the Argonauts' fame) sailed past the Sirens, the story goes that Orpheus successfully chanted a counter melody to protect his companions. When another great 'hero' Odysseus passed Thassos on his way back from the Trojan War, he had his comrades stuff their ears with wax so they would not hear the Sirens. Odysseus however, had himself tied to the mast so that he could safely listen to their beautiful songs. The Sirens sang as they approached, their words apparently where even more enticing than the melody. Odysseus' heart was filled with longing, but the ropes held him and the ship quickly sailed to safer waters. It was predicted in the myths, that the Sirens would die when a ship passed them unharmed and since both the Argonauts and Odysseus succeeded in escaping, the reason that no one has seen them since, could be that they are dead and gone!

One of the many erotic adventures of Zeus, the supreme god of the ancient Greeks, explains the mythological naming of Thassos. The story goes that Agenor who was King of Eastern Phoenicia, had four sons, Phoenix, Cilix, Cadmus and Thassos and one daughter, Europa. One spring day, Zeus transformed himself into a bull, kidnapped the buxom Europa and carried her on his back to the Dictaean Cave in Crete. There, in the form of a handsome eagle, Zeus coupled with Europa, and from that sacred union three sons were born: Minos, the famous King of Crete, Rhadamanthys, the wise lawgiver, and Sarpedon, the first King of Lycia. Europa, knowing that her father disapproved of the union, hid from him in Crete, whilst continuing to enjoy Zeus's favours.

Agenor enraged at this, ordered his sons to look high and low for Europa and not to return unless they found her. Phoenix set out towards the south, Cilix went north until he reached a fertile land where he made himself king, since then it has been known as Cilicia. Cadmus, after unsuccessfully searching through the Greek islands, continued his quest on mainland Greece. He visited the Oracle of Apollo at Delphi and consulted the Pythian priestess. Although he followed her advice, he was still unable to find Europa. After passing through Phocis, he came to Boeotia, where he built an acropolis, Cadmeia, and below it a town with broad avenues, naming it Thebes. Thassos searched for Europa in various places until he came to an island off Thrace. Captivated by its marvellous climate and lush vegetation and unable to return to his father without Europa, he gave up his quest. Thassos and his retinue settled on the island, which has borne his name ever since.

Herodotus confirms this story, by writing in his work 'Histories', that "the island is called after that Phoenician Thassos." Other ancient writers give the island descriptive names such as Aeria (cool summer breezes). As previously mentioned, the latter name was mentioned in the Delphic Oracle received by the leader of the Parian colonists, Telesicles (680 B.C.): "Tell the Parians, Telesicles, that I have ordered you to build on the isle of Aeria a great city that will be visible from all around." Further known descriptive names include Aethria, meaning 'clear blue sky', and Chrysia, a reference to the lustrous gleam of the gold (in Greek chrysos) mined on the island.

Religious belief of the Thassians, as with all the ancient Greeks, was centred on the twelve gods of Olympus. The island's patron was Heracles, a mystical god who according to some may have had his origins not in the Greek half-god Heracles (Hercules), but in the Phoenician god Melkarth. Special honours were also reserved for the god of the sea Poseidon and the goddess of the hunt

Artemis. Dionysus, the god of wine, together with his Satyrs (the chief one being Silenus) and the Maenads*, were worshiped in orgiastic rites. The mysteries of Demeter, brought to Thassos by the Parian priestess Cleobia, were among other rites celebrated by the inhabitants. There were special feasts of Pythian Apollo**, whose snowy white temple sparkled on the acropolis above Thassos Town (Limenas).

Hippocrates (460 - circa 370 B.C.), known as the father of modern medicine, lived on Thassos for more than three years and wrote extensively about the island and its people. These texts have been important in confirming such facts as the ancient place names, the position and use of buildings, the health of the islanders and the annual weather at that time.

**In Greek mythology, Maenads were female worshippers of Dionysus, the god of mystery, wine and intoxication (equivalent to the Roman god Bacchus). Their name literally translates as 'raving ones'. They were known as wild, insane women who could not be reasoned with....no comment! The mysteries of Dionysus inspired the women to ecstatic frenzy; they indulged in copious amounts of violence, bloodletting, sexual activity, wild dancing and heavy drinking. They were usually pictured as wearing diadems of vine leaves, clothed in fawnskins and carrying the thyrsus. The Maenads are the most significant members of the Thiasus, the retinue of Dionysus.*

***Apollo's chief oracular shrine was at Delphi, which he was said to have seized, while still an infant, by killing its guardian the serpent Python. This event was celebrated every four years in the festival of the Pythia. Other festivals held in Apollo's honour included the Carneia, Daphnephoria and the yearly Thargelia and Pyanepsia, which celebrated spring and autumn respectively.*

Greek periods (B.C.)

Archaic	720 – 480
Classical	480 – 323
Hellenistic	323 – 27

Culture

For those who have not visited Greece before, how can I explain the Greek people and their culture? It could be said that their way of life reflects many of the positive attributes of the UK in the not so distant past, but now sadly disappearing. These include a high level of respect for the individual, the family and the community, a belief that the quality of life is more important than the quantity and a strong self-reliance, rather than an increasing dependence on the state.

All I will say is that I find the Greeks very honest (especially on the islands), sincere and extremely friendly and one of my greatest hopes is that the ever-increasing exposure to the tourist trade does not devalue, or corrupt these virtues.

Many of the locals have two separate lives, the first during the holiday season, working in one of the many service industries dedicated to the tourist industry. Then once the tourists have left, another that is more reminiscent of the past life on the island, which includes amongst others, employment in agriculture, fishing and community services.

You will find that, as in many Mediterranean countries, much of the day-to-day activities start very early, then stop at lunchtime and reconvene early evening, continuing late into the night. So expect many of the shops and other services to be closed for a few hours in the afternoon. Remember the old adage 'only mad dogs and Englishmen go out in the midday sun! Though there are no mad ones, you will see some wandering the streets, but they all seem to wear collars and are very friendly, if not entirely appreciated by the owners of the tavernas. One of the most loveable and good-natured is 'Popi' who lives in Thassos Town, she is white and beige with a high proportion of Beagle in her.

During your stay, one of the simplest ways of saying thank you (Efharisto), is to take time to learn a few basic Greek words and phrases. I can assure you that even though the majority of Thassians speak at least a little English, it will be much appreciated by them. To that end, I have added a glossary of frequently used Greek words and phrases at the end of this book.

Beyond the tourist

With the first drops of rain another summer season comes to a close. The days get shorter and the sunsets are a deeper red and purple. A line of small fishing boats appear on the horizon every sunset fishing for squid, for this is the season when shoals of them arrive off the coast of Thassos. The Meltemi winds (the Aegean equivalent of the French Mistral) appear in the evenings. There is a fresher feel in the air; reminding all on the island that winter is approaching.

The warm sunny weather though continues for the whole of September. At the first sign of the autumn leaf fall, a new urgency is in the air, the tourists may be leaving, but this is a busy time for the Thassians. Autumn is the time to gather the grape harvest, which must be pressed to produce the famous Thassian wine and Tsipouro. Tsipouro is a strong distilled spirit (a pomace brandy), containing approximately 45% alcohol by volume and is produced from the residues of the wine pressing. In the southern Aegean it tends to be known as Raki, which is a little stronger. Restaurants usually serve it in shot-glasses, very cold, often with a meze of walnuts, raisins, almonds, feta cheese, olives, or alternatively accompanying halva or other desserts.

The wines are produced first and then the Tsipouro must be distilled from what is left from the pressing. On Thassos, you will find many that use their grape harvest solely to produce a fine Tsipouro.

Almost every family has at least a small vineyard somewhere on the island. It is a backbreaking job, which marks the beginning of at least two months of hard work for most of the islanders. Whole families, including the children join in to help each other collect the grapes. After they have all been collected, they are brought home and placed in cisterns, or half barrels. In past years, the grapes were trampled by foot to free the juice, but today machines are used to crush most grapes. Those families that will make wine will place the juice into wine barrels for the fermentation process. All the leftovers are collected and placed in other barrels to ferment for several weeks. Then this is distilled to extract small quantities of Tsipouro.

Those that choose not to make wine, take their crushed grapes and the juice and place them into barrels to start the fermentation process. Nothing else is added, and the only work necessary is to stir the barrels every few days. After several weeks it will be distilled to extract large quantities of Tsipouro.

Families on Thassos continue to produce this drink in the traditional way as their fathers and grandfathers have done before them. They have to obtain a licence, which permits them to use the communal distillery for a pre-booked period. The pressed grapes that have already fermented for several weeks are placed in one of the distillery's large copper cauldrons, and the top is sealed. A fire is lit under the cauldron and the resulting steam escapes through a copper pipe, which exits from the lid of the cauldron and passes through a condenser filled with cold water where the vapour condenses into Tsipouro.

This is a fun time on the island and is celebrated by the tasting of the new Tsipouro......sometimes too much! The distillery operates non-stop day and night; the nightly vigil livened by singing, eating and story telling. Drop by drop the Tsipouro is collected and stored in glass demijohns (large narrow-necked bottles). It is a pure and strong drink with a very slight aniseed taste, but with no morning after effects.... or that's what they say.

Olive picking

The olive picking season starts in early November. The hills and mountains all around the island of Thassos come alive with the sights and sounds of families collecting the olives, as they have done for generations. The men beat the olives down from the trees using long sticks, whilst the women and children pick them up either by hand, or in large nets spread under the olive trees. When the olives have been gathered, those not destined for eating whole are taken to the olive press, where they are pressed to extract the famous Thassos olive oil. The first oil of the season is the best and is used for salads, etc., whilst the old oil from last year is reserved for frying, or for lighting the icon lamps in the churches.

Only in mid December can the people of Thassos slow down and start preparing for Christmas.

Carnivals and religious events

New Year's Day - The Pomegranate and the Goblins

Since olden times on Thassos, the night of New Year's Eve sees families gathering around the fireplace. They traditionally throw some olive leaves onto the fire, making wishes and saying prayers for the New Year. Later on, they set the table, on which there is always curdled milk, 'saragli' pastry and honey with walnuts. The main course is traditionally goat's head casserole with onions and of course the Santa Claus pie. It is a long standing custom for the Thassian housewives to form pictures of everyday life, such as houses, animals, flowers, etc on the Santa Claus pie.

On New Year's Day the families take a pomegranate with them to church and when they came back home, they crack it on the doorstep to disperse the seeds and bring good luck and abundance. On this day, people open the doors of their house (but only to the relatives they consider to be lucky). These are the first visitors, carrying a heavy stone and welcoming in the New Year by singing the phrase "everything kakaka and one koukoukou, everything kakaka and one koukoukou, let the bag of the householder be as heavy as this stone", which means may the flocks of sheep give birth to lots and lots of females (everything = kakaka) and only a few males (one = koukoukou).

The festive cycle traditionally comes to an end on the third day after the Epiphany (the day when traditionally the 'Three Wise Men' visited the baby Jesus), then families light a fire in the fireplace to help scare off the Goblins.

'August, Mr. August'

August, generous as always and abundant in different kinds of sweet fruits, has always been the favourite month of the year for the locals and its arrival has been celebrated with open-air fires, dances and songs almost everywhere in Greece. The skipping over the fire, which traditionally takes place on the last day of July and is accompanied by the folk song 'August, Mr. August, with figs and walnuts and red grapes' is a praise to the hottest month of the summer, but at the same time a purification from diseases and germs, which were easily spread in the past, due to the high temperatures. Recently, people have revived this custom in many villages on Thassos, such as Kalivia, Limenaria and Potos. In Kazaviti, after the 'skipping over the fire', the inhabitants offer 'koulbani', along with two age-old local dishes, 'tatarika' (a variety of vegetables cooked in olive oil) and beans with 'pepper-cabbages', which are pickled vegetables preserved in vinegar and spices.

Thassian wedding ceremony

The reconstruction of the Thassian wedding ceremony is one of the favourite folklore shows during the summer, not only for the locals, but also for the visitors to Thassos. The Cultural Society 'Hatzigjorgis' has been staging the show in August in Theologos since 1978, succeeding in attracting more than 2,500 visitors every year and so giving a boost to life in the picturesque village. In the past, the preparations for a wedding were started well in advance of the actual day. The bridal gown had to be clean and ironed and this meant extra work for almost every young girl in the village.

On the wedding day, before the bride got dressed, her mother would take her to the next room and place a piece of fishing net over the bride to ward off the 'evil eye'. Then shortly before the bridegroom appeared, the girls of the village would give the bride the last advice in song: "Are you listening, my little bride? Listen to what we shall order for you, so as to stand as a pigeon, to bow as a twig, to blush as a red carnation..."

In the meantime, the bridegroom gets dressed in another house and then sets off to first collect the best man and then the bride, to the accompaniment of musicians. But the girls who are at the bride's house lock the bridegroom outside and ask for a promise. Only when the promise is satisfactory, do they open the door and sing to him: "My bridegroom, please, do us a favour, so not wither the rose we give you..."

In the meantime, the residents who are outside the bride's house have already started dancing. Then to the accompaniment of a band, they all set off together for the church. In the front row, there are the mules decorated with talismans and white handkerchiefs and the whole dowry of the bride and there are the girls who are holding her embroideries and dresses.

On this day, the whole village is decorated and there are colourful hand-woven fabrics hanging from the balconies of the houses. Nowadays, after the church service, the ceremonial procession crosses the picturesque narrow streets of the village and arrives at the football field. Here people continue to celebrate with dancing, singing and drinking. There are of course plenty of treats for the guests, local ouzo, roasted goat's meat and 'Saragli' pastry to name but a few.

Carnival customs

The residents of the village of Panagia have revived an ancient carnival event, which now takes place every year in the village, forty days before Easter (the most important event in the religious year). The local folklore association 'Bacchus', named after the Greek god (Dionysus in Roman mythology) organises this comic event, which has many elements that celebrate this unusual ancient god. During the carnival, a group of participants in multi-coloured attire, having the male phallus and vine leaf as symbols, take part in caustic satire, jokes and mocking poems. Throughout the proceedings, red wine that was seen as a gift of the god Dionysus, flows in abundance. The carnival floats, after negotiating the picturesque narrow streets of Panagia, enter the square to perform a 'street play', commenting sarcastically on the local as well as worldwide current affairs.

The carnival is also celebrated with a procession of floats in Potamia, with theatrical performances full of vivid local colour in Kallirachi and with the burning of the 'King of Carnival' in Rachoni. On Shrove Monday, people in Theologos organize shows and competitions including traditional kite flying.

Principle festival and holiday dates during 2008

March 9th	Carnival in Potamia
March 10th	Carnival in Panagia
April 27th	Orthodox Easter Sunday
May 1st	May Day
May 15th *	Assumption Day (Panagia and Maries)
June 16th	Holy Spirit Day (major festival)
July/August	Various festivals around the island
August 6th *	Transfiguration Day (Sotiras)
August 15th	The Assumption of the Virgin Mary in Panagia and Rachoni
August 29th	Festival in Agios Ioannis

I would recommend that you confirm the details of the festival and that the date has not changed. Those marked with an asterisk are approximate, as their dates have not been confirmed at the time of going to press. Many of the above are interesting to see and even take part in. To give you an idea, 'The Assumption of the Virgin Mary' in Panagia, is a huge festival with a church service that is followed at 11:00 a.m. by a colourful parade through the village.

Local products

Marble

Thassos is renowned for its snow-white marble, exporting the product all over the world.

From the 6th century B.C., Thassos marble was exported to Samothrace and other islands, the coast of Asia Minor and to southern Greece where it was used to construct temples and other impressive buildings. From the 1st century B.C. until the 3rd century A.D., Thassos marble was imported extensively by the Romans, who prized the high quality white stone. You can see an example of an ancient marble quarry at Aliki (see Aliki under 'Archaeological sites on Thassos').

Marble is still extensively worked on the island, with major quarries just outside Thassos Town in the Vathy and Panagia regions. During your visit to Thassos, you may hear the explosions from the workings and if you are interested there are free guided tours of the quarry.

Honey

Honey is one of the main products of Thassos, confirmed by the number of shops and stalls all over the island selling the local product. As you travel around the island you will also see the many brightly coloured beehives lining the roads and forests.

The honeybees collect the nectar and pollen from the pine and fir tree flowers and the herbs and flowers of Thassos, producing a distinctive blonde and aromatic honey.

Thassos since antiquity has been a centre of apiculture in Greece and today many thousands of kilos of honey are produced each year. Between Skala Prinos and Skala Rachoni is the Thassos Apiarist Co-operative factory (the co-operative has over 100 members), which stores, packs, sells and distributes the honey. The co-operative's objective is to select the honey from the beekeepers of Thassos, quality control production and distribute the final product around the island, as well as supplying a flourishing export trade.

Visitors are always welcomed at the factory, to tour the works and taste the honey. With regard to buying honey as a souvenir or present, you may be told that there are restrictions in taking it back into the UK. However, I have checked with H.M. Customs and DEFRA and as Greece is a member of the EU, there is no restriction.

Olives

The island's fertile soil means that Thassos is the greatest olive oil producing region of northern Greece after Halkidiki. Those farmed on Thassos are low tree varieties that crop heavily and give both high quality light coloured oil and delicious edible black olives. A quick tip.....the bags of local olives that can be purchased in the supermarkets can be quite salty for some people's taste, so it may be better opting for the variety in jars.

Wine

In antiquity the wines of Macedonia and mainly those of Thassos, were exported to the whole of the known world. The quality of Thassian wines was celebrated by many famous ancient writers, who commented on their excellence and individuality. However, with the Roman domination of the Mediterranean, the centre of wine production shifted from the northern to the southern Aegean, and finally away from Greece altogether.

Wine is still produced on the island, but the number of vineyards has radically decreased since antiquity, which means that wine is no longer a major product of Thassos.

Timber

Although the industry has declined over the years, timber is still produced from the abundant pine and fir forests on the island.

Local animals

Sheep and goats

Whilst sheep and goat rearing is not a major farming activity on Thassos, on your travels you will see large numbers (especially goats) in certain regions and it is obvious that the resulting meat and milk is an important addition to the island's food production. The majority of livestock farming is in the central and eastern regions around Kazaviti, Theologos, Panagia and Potamia.

Poultry

Chickens are reared free-range on the island and one thing I can say having been used to factory farmed varieties in the UK, is that they taste wonderful especially when they are cooked on a rotisserie in the Greek way.

Dogs and cats

There are many cats on the island (most seem to be feral) and a few dogs wandering free, the latter all seem to wear collars, so I presume they have owners. Both though are very friendly and pose no problem, except for the taverna staff that favour chasing them off, mainly for the sake of the diners.

Wild animals

For those interested in wildlife (the animal type), I have added the following information:

Apart from the odd feral goat and cat, wild mammals are scarce and inconspicuous on the island. Especially at night, the occasional brown rat can be seen scurrying across the road, or scavenging near to waste bins. At dusk, bats can be seen swooping through the evening sky feeding on the myriad of insects. The occasional dead hedgehog on the road, especially in the north, bares testament to their presence and in addition, stone martens and brown hares are resident on the island.

Greece reportedly supports ninety-five species of land mammals and the proximity of Thassos to the mainland, suggests that it should share in this diversity. Research has identified a distribution of twenty-five species of rodent across Greece, just four species in total have been reported from the Aegean islands, namely the lesser mole rat, the broad-toothed field mouse, the brown rat and the house mouse. Two rare bat species, the horseshoe and the long-fingered bat are apparently present on the island, with a report of a large bat roost in the Drakotrypa cave near Panagia.

In 2005 there were sightings of two shrews, apparently one had been liberated from a hotel swimming pool in Thassos Town (no, I don't know why a shrew was in a swimming pool) and the other was found dead in Megalo Kazaviti.

Birds

There is a wide variety of bird life on the island (surprising as the locals shoot them), including the common sparrow, which you will find are very tame, partridge, woodcock, wood pigeon and mainly in the south, migratory quails. There is also a wide variety of owls (their calls are a familiar sound during the night) and an impressive range of birds of prey. Marine birds include seagulls, shearwaters, shags, cormorants and heron and especially in the winter, the island plays host to Caribbean flamingos, swans and many species of duck.

Herons

One sight to look out for if you are travelling from Alexander the Great Airport to Keramoti, are the massive heron nests along the way which are perched high on buildings or in trees and the herons themselves feeding in the marshes that line the road.

The ferries and the seagulls

One of the fascinating sights when travelling to Thassos is whilst on the ferry to and from the island. The local seagull population have learnt that not only does the ferry disgorge fish in its wake, providing them with an easy meal, but that they can also be guaranteed of further easy pickings from the passengers.

Throughout the journey the seagulls swoop and hover along the length of the ferry, catching morsels of bread, biscuits etc. that are thrown overboard, or more amazingly plucked from the hands of those who have the courage to hold the food out. So if you want to experience this first-hand, take some food with you on the trip and make sure you count your fingers afterwards!

On Panagia island just off the southern tip of Thassos is the largest colony of seagulls in the Mediteranneаn.

Dolphins

Although dolphins are to be found in the whole of the Mediterranean, they are a relatively rare sight in open waters. However, in 2006 a pod was seen to 'play' in the bow wake of the ferries travelling to and from Thassos and in May this year two were seen off the Eros II excursion boat. So keep an eye out, you may just be lucky.

Sponges

Look in any gift shop on Thassos and it is almost certain you will see sponges for sale as souvenirs and it has to be remembered that these are the remains of a marine animal, not a plant.

Getting there

Package holidays

The first and obvious way of visiting Thassos is by booking through a tour operator. The three major UK companies that are offering holidays on Thassos in 2008 are:-

Kosmar - Friday flights
Portland Direct - Sunday flights
Thomson (TUI) - Sunday flights

A la carte

Flight only

Here I have covered three main options. The first is by way of the tour companies, who usually offer flight-only alternatives. To give you an idea, one major tour operator charges around £215.00 p.p. return from Birmingham/Manchester into Alexander the Great Airport (near Keramoti).

From the airport you need to take a taxi or bus to either Keramoti (13 km and 10 euro by taxi), where you can board a ferry to Limenas (Thassos Town), or to Kavala (35 km and 15 euro by taxi), from where there is a ferry service to Skala Prinos (northwest of the island) or hydrofoils to Limenas and Skala Prinos (see information regarding the hydrofoil services on page 119).

It is advisable to book flights early as you may find prices rising towards your travel date, or the seats are fully booked/reserved for their package customers.

Three internet sites that we have found very user friendly for finding discount flights are:-

www.skyscanner.net

www.charterflights.co.uk

www.cheapflights.co.uk

The second alternative is to fly into Thessaloniki and travel on to Kavala. The most cost effective way is by bus, with the fare working out at about 15 euro per person. The bus from the airport into Thessaloniki in summertime departs every 15 - 30 minutes and in wintertime every 30 - 45 minutes. The bus, number 78, goes from the airport (in front of the check-in-hall) to the bus terminus in the centre of Thessaloniki and takes about 45 minutes. From here you can transfer to the bus that will take you direct to Kavala.

Alternatively you can also take a taxi from the airport to the bus terminus, this takes about 30 minutes. You will find the taxis in front of the international and national arrival building. I would suggest that you confirm the price before you go.

At the Thessaloniki bus terminus you have two choices:

You can take the bus to Kavala that departs on the hour (between 06:00 and 20:00) and goes via the mountains taking approx. 3 hours. Or you can take the bus that departs at either 09:00, 12:00, 15:00 and 18:00 and goes via Nea Peramos, taking around 2 hours.

All the buses terminate in Kavala near the ferryboat and hydrofoil ports. Information and prices for the ferries and hydrofoil can be found in the chapter on 'Getting around'.

Another option if you want to be more independent, is to hire a car from Thessaloniki airport for the trip to Kavala, or for the full duration of your holiday. Prices vary dependant on the model, length of hire and the time of year and of course the car hire company.

The road from Thessaloniki to Kavala is motorway most of the way, a few kilometres about half way along the route is still single carriageway, the section to complete the motorway is under construction now and should be open by 2008. The drive from the airport to either the Kavala or Keramoti ferry terminals (both opposite the island), will take about 2½ to 3 hours not including stops and is a pleasant journey.

The third alternative is to fly into Athens, from where you can either take Helenic Railways from Athens to Drama (9½ hrs) and then by bus to Kavala, or alternatively an internal flight from Athens to Kavala (Olympic, or Aegean), which costs from around £60 p.p.

The two main scheduled flight carriers from the UK to both Athens and Thessaloniki are BA and Easyjet. You can check prices, departure airports and times on their websites, the addresses are:-

www.britishairways.com

www.easyjet.com

By road

The distance by road between the south coast of Britain and Kavala is approx. 3,000 km. One direct route takes you through Belgium, Germany, Austria, Hungary, Romania, Bulgaria and then into northern Greece and down to Kavala. A non-stop trip (two drivers) will take approx. 50hrs, but of course this depends on whether you decide to take toll motorways, or side roads and the speed at which you drive. A reasonably relaxed drive with night stops should take approx. 3½ - 4 days.

If you decide to take this option, I would advise that you do a little homework (best on the internet) regarding the rules and regulations of driving through the countries on your route, or talk to someone who has recently completed a similar trip.

Hotels, studios and apartments

As you can appreciate there is a vast selection of holiday accommodation on the island, from the deluxe such as the Lido and Amfipolis hotels in Thassos Town and the Enavlion hotel in Golden Beach, all the way down to simple studios.

Whilst I could write a book just on accommodation, my advice would be (if you want to book beforehand) do your homework by obtaining a range of tour company brochures to decide on the resort and then search the web. As they say, one of the most important points is "location, location, location." If you want that quiet relaxing holiday, you don't want to be above a taverna and if you like the nightlife, you don't want to be in the middle of nowhere.

One point I believe is less important is for your accommodation to offer a restaurant service. One of the joys of Thassos, is to visit the vast choice of tavernas and restaurants on the island and enjoy what can invariably be attractive surroundings and good food. Who wants to frequent a hotel restaurant, when you can sit by the sea and watch the sun set over the Aegean. If you have a family, you will find that the Greek culture is very family orientated and therefore children are welcomed and catered for by restaurant staff. Most tavernas offer breakfast, either continental or English.

One thing I can confirm is that without exception, the accommodation I have stayed in within Greece in the last 30 years has always been clean and good value for money. You may find that at the 'budget' end of the market, things can be a bit basic as far as room facilities are concerned. However, the top end of the market is as good as anything you will get back in the UK and for a lot less!

Most apartments and studios will have at least a two-ring stove, a fridge and basic cutlery, pots and pans and utensils, a double or two single beds with side cupboards and a wardrobe (with never enough hangers). Usually there is only a shower (not a bath) with a W.C. For those who like a good nights sleep, it may be advisable if you are visiting in the high season, to select accommodation that has air-conditioning. Telephones and televisions in accommodation are usually to be found at the 'higher end' of the market.

One strange but positive anomaly I have noticed in the past, is that room cleaning and laundry changes occur more regularly than is specified in the brochure or room information. You should also find that when the odd problem such as a blocked sink or faulty light occurs, a quick talk with the management will invariably result in a quick resolution to the problem.

An alternative to booking from home, is to take a flight to Kavala (Alexander the Great Airport), catch the ferry and look for your accommodation when you arrive on Thassos. You will find there is always some accommodation available and at most times you can negotiate a good price. In Thassos Town, as with the other main resorts, there are a number of property companies who may have suitable accommodation on their books, or go to the Tourist Police office and they can help point you in the right direction (page 168).

In the new ferry port in Thassos Town there is a kiosk run by the island's hotel association where you can also check hotel availability.

If you would like further help, please refer to the 'Concierge Service' at the back of this book.

Camping

For those who enjoy the 'back to nature' style holiday, or are looking for a 'budget' way of visiting Thassos, there are six main campsites on the island. All the campsites are good, with shaded areas to set up your tent (or on some sites you can hire one of the permanent tents). Amenities usually include a cafe, a supermarket, a restaurant or bar (with usually others nearby) and some have a nightclub. Almost all of them are a few steps from a beach.

The campsites are, clockwise around the island from Thassos Town:-

Golden Beach:

Chryssia Ammoudia
Panagia
Thassos 640 04
Tel: 25930-61207, 61472 (and 3)
Tax: 61949
Owner: Chryssi Ammoudia Tourist Enterprises
Manager: George Matzanis
Open: May - October

Potos:

Paradissos
Potos
Thassos 640 02
Tel: 25930-51950, 51906
Owner: Vassilikou Tourist Enterprises
Manager: Ms Elsa Vlachou Vassilikou
Open: May - October

Limenaria:

Pefkari
Limenaria
Thassos 640 02
Tel: 25930-51190, 51595
Manager: E. Manderis
Open: April - October
Skala Sotiras:

Dedalos (I think they need to change their name!)
Skala Sotiras
Thassos 640 04
Tel: 25930-71365 (6 and 7)
Fax: 71365
Owner: Markopoulos S.A.
Manager: Markos Botsos
Open: May - September 25th

Skala Prinos:

Prino
Skala Prinos
Thassos 640 10
Tel: 25930-71171 (2 and 3)
Managed by: NGTO
Manager: S. Mesaritakis
Open: May - October

Skala Rachoni:

Perseus
Skala Rachoni
Thassos 640 04
Tel: 25930-81242
Manager: P. Stergioudis
Open: May - October

Things to do

Places to visit

Inland

I have to be honest and say that I have been a little disappointed during my visits to some of the inland villages. Other than experiencing a more Greek approach to life than that on the coast, they have little *in my view* to offer. The occasional festival or carnival held in the villages, does make them worth a visit at that time, but I believe the other attractions and coastal villages (described in the chapter on 'Beaches and resorts') on the island are more interesting and rewarding. Below I have listed (going clockwise from Thassos Town) the inland villages that I personally believe are worthy of a visit.

Panagia

One village that I do recommend for a visit is Panagia, which was the capital of the island in the 19th century. Both attractive and interesting, Panagia has numerous small streams (emanating from natural springs further up the mountain), little pools and waterfalls, that form attractive features throughout the village. There is a local tradition that if you drink from the fountain in Panagia, you will never want to leave. Most of the houses of Panagia are traditional ones, with covered balconies, schist roofs and adorned internally with wood.

There are a number of tavernas and local shops (many selling souvenirs), most near the centre. The village church, built in 1832 and dedicated to the Virgin Mary is imposing and worthy of a visit. Panagia is famous for its spoon sweets, walnuts, figs and tomatoes.

If you are driving, I would suggest you park just before you enter the village from Thassos Town (next to the 'Panorama' café, run by Graham and Angie, a very friendly expat couple from England). From here you can take in the magnificent views of the bay below.

Potamia

Potamia is known locally not only for its animal rearing, but also for beans and the chestnuts from the local trees. The main attraction in Potamia is the museum of Polygnotos Vagis. Born on Thassos in 1892, he left the island at the age of 19 to emigrate to America. Renowned as a sculptor, on his death he bequeathed his works to the Greek government on the understanding that a museum dedicated to his work would be created in his village.

Convent of Archangelou Michael

I have added the convent in this section, as it is one of the attractions you will pass if you are travelling round the island on the coast road. The convent is situated roughly halfway between Aliki and Astris and is dedicated to the patron saint of the island. The stop is well worth the time, if only for the wonderful views from its imposing position clinging to the cliffs above the bay.

There is a small admission charge and if you are wearing such as shorts and a tee shirt, you will be asked to 'cover up' with a supplied smock. Within the walls you will find beautifully kept gardens exploding with colour.

Theologos

A myriad of alleys criss-cross this mountain settlement, opening into small picturesque squares. Old mansions line the alleys and squares, such as that of Chadjigeorgis Metaxas, who was president of the island and leader of the unsuccessful independence revolt in 1821. You will find tavernas, coffee bars, shops and a number of interesting churches. There is a small folklore museum which houses costumes and artefacts from daily life in the past. Theologos is the setting for a number of events during the year.

Maries

The drive up to Maries is picturesque and scenic and the village is quaint and unspoilt with what is purported to be the oldest church on Thassos, a small river runs below the village. Lake Marion, situated just past Maries is worth a visit, but only if you have a high ground clearance 4WD as the road is a dirt track and is unadvisable in anything else.

Sotiras

Sotiras is located between Kalirachi and Prinos. It is a mountain village built at an altitude of 380 metres, on the foothills of Mount Ypsario, which offers some wonderful views.

Today Sotiras only has a few inhabitants, but the ancient ruins, old, traditional houses, beautiful ancient churches and a picturesque fountain dating from 1888, all these make the village well worth the drive.

Kazaviti (Mikro and Megalo Prinos)

Now here there is a little confusion, so I will try and simplify. Going inland and up from Prinos, after 4 km you will come to a number of villages that really merge into one. The first village you come to (and I would suggest you pass by) is Mikro Prinos. Just outside the village on your right you will see a waterfall and if you feel like a walk, this is a perfect place to stop. If you continue you will soon enter Megalo Prinos, but this is also for all intent and purposes Kazaviti. A short, but steep hill on the right leads you into the village square, circled by tavernas and cafes (I would suggest you park carefully away from the square, as in summer this is filled with their tables and chairs).

These are the oldest villages in the area, perched in the mountains and hidden amongst forest and lush greenery. The villages contain some beautiful houses, many with what looks like an Alpine influence, with their traditional wooden balconies, stonewalls and painted ceilings. A resident German has put great effort into protecting and conserving these beautiful villages and it is worthy of a visit to view his success.

Archaeological sites

Although there are numerous archaeological sites on Thassos, many are poorly presented and some are even surrounded with wire fences and padlocked gates. In this book, I will try to differentiate between those worthy of a visit and those that you may find disappointing. I will however suggest, for those hardened amateur archaeologists with a good imagination, keep your eyes peeled as you travel the island for the brown 'archaeological site' signs and good hunting. One final request, please respect all the archaeological sites, they are more fragile than they appear.

I have split the archaeological sites into those in Limenas (which I have further split into two main groupings) and those on the rest of the island. I would suggest that the two groupings in Limenas (Thassos Town) could be seen on separate days, especially when the temperature is high (see map on page 179).

Archaeological sites in Limenas - **Group one**

Agora

The first and most important site on the island is the agora, situated in Limenas next to the old harbour. This complex was the heart of the ancient city and was enclosed within the city walls; during excavations, the foundations of buildings were found that dated back to the 6th century B.C. Walk along the harbour road and if you look carefully you can see the remains of the ancient naval harbour walls beneath the water.

With the harbour on your left and the taverna 'Symi' just in front of you, on your right up a few steps you will see a small square, behind which is located the island's archaeological museum. In the summer of 2008 major renovations and extensions to the museum should be completed, which will place it as one of the most important museums in Greece. Displays will include Pre-historic, Archaic, Greek and Roman exhibition galleries presenting a wide range of finds from the island. There will also be galleries that present the history and socio-economic past of the island. All of this makes the museum a 'must' to visit.

As you face the museum, to your left is the agora (the Greek equivalent of the Roman forum), with law courts, official offices, open-meeting areas and commercial buildings. Through the gate and down a few steps you enter the ruins of the agora, which were first excavated between 1948 and 1955 and are approximately 2.5 metres below the modern ground level. As you enter the agora you will see in front and to the right, an information board with a map and details of the buildings and history (also see page 180).

The agora was a trapezoid area approx. 80 x 100 m, surrounded in the northwest, southwest and southeast by long arcades (stoas) that were ornamented with statues, altars and sacred places. In the middle of the agora, stood the miracle-working statue of Theagenis where animal sacrifices and offerings were made by his devotees to obtain the cures that the statue was said to bestow (the three tiered circular base and sacrifice tethering ring are still visible). Theagenis was one of the most praised Thassians, who won over 1,200 athletic crowns, amongst them the Pankration* in 476 B.C. and the boxing title at the Olympic Games in 480 B.C. (the same month as the Battle of Thermopylae).

Just inside the entrance on the left you will see a semi-circular stone seat (exedra). This and the area in front are the remains of the Roman law courts of Thassos. Turn left and walk behind the stone seat, down what was the northwestern colonnaded stoa.

* The Pankration was an event that was a gruelling combination of boxing and wrestling. Punches were allowed, but the rules outlawed biting and gouging an opponent's eyes, nose, or mouth with fingernails (although these were known to occur). Attacks such as kicking an opponent in the belly, which are against the rules in modern sports, were perfectly legal.

Prytaneum, Artemision and Dionysion

As you turn right at the end of the stoa, on your left are the remains of what was most probably the Prytaneum (an ancient city's government building). Fronting the Prytaneum was the sanctuary of Zeus Agoraios and further southeast, the law courts, workshops, storerooms and a short stoa.

The rear of the southeast stoa was lined with shops that opened onto the 'Great Main Road', a small section of which is still visible today in the far right corner of the agora. This road directly linked the Dionysion, the Heraclion and the gate of 'Zeus and Hera' and indirectly to the other southern gates. If you walk down the 'Great Main Road', you will find on the left the well-preserved remains of an exedra, dated to the 1st century A.D and by a sculptor named Limendes. A few metres further down on the left is a passage, which takes you to the 'Odeum', a small theatre that was the venue for such events as simple plays, music and poetry recitals and religious performances.

At this point it is worth taking time to wander around the site, which is extensive. When you have finished, walk to the back far left of the agora, here you will see a path (the passage of Theoroi) that leads under a small bridge, behind the three erect columns. On its walls were engraved marvelous bas-reliefs of Apollo with the Nymphs, the Graces holding in their raised hands proffers of wreaths and fruits, Hermes and others, all of which were discovered in 1863 by E. Miller, a French traveller, and taken by him to the Louvre Museum in Paris. Next to the passage is the tomb of Glaukos, the famous Parian general who accompanied Telesicles on his second military expedition to Thassos in the early 7th century B.C. (page 7). Now take the path under the bridge and on your right you will find an ancient communal well (one of three in this area, dating from the archaic to Byzantine periods). Behind it are the ruins of the Artemision, the temple to Artemis. Continuing down the path you come to the area that was excavated in 2006 (the archaeological report has not yet been published).

After covering all in the agora, return to the entrance, exit and walk down to the harbour and turn right walking past the Symi taverna. In front you will see the Patrikos taverna, up the hill to the right of the taverna you will find the Dionysion, the sanctuary of Dionysus, the prime god of theatre. This sanctuary is situated at the bottom of the passage that in antiquity led up to the theatre. It was built in the 4th century B.C. and originally had an enclosing wall with two entrances (much of which is still covered by the modern buildings). In front of the raised podium and to the left of the marble stairs that led up to the entrance of the sanctuary, you can see two sacrificial altars, one archaic (which bares a later 4th century B.C. inscription) and one dated to the 5th or 4th century B.C.

Northern gates, archaic quarter and Posideio

From the Dionysion, return down the hill, turning right behind the multi-chimney two-storey building that faces onto the sea. This road passes just behind the course of the ancient city walls that in this section had three gates opening onto the harbours. One gate is lost, the first remaining gate (100 metres down on the left) is 'the Goddess on the Chariot' dated to the late 5th or early 4th century B.C. You will see depicted on the pillar, the female figure of Artemis standing on her chariot, drawn by two horses and with the bearded figure of Hermes standing next to the horses holding the bridles.

Past this gate on the right, you will come to the ruins of the 'Sanctuary of Poseidon' (Poseidonion). The central court of the sanctuary was reached by large double-doors, the court contained a circular base (possibly for an altar) and colonnades with rooms facing into the centre. During excavations within the sanctuary, an elegant Hellenistic statuette was found, depicting the goddess Aphrodite sitting on a dolphin's back with a small Eros perched on its tail. This statuette is exhibited in the Thassos Archaeological Museum next to the agora site.

Walk down the road a little further and on your right you will see the ruins of the archaic quarter (North Quarter), continuously inhabited from archaic times to the late Roman period and nearly opposite is the second gate in this section of the wall, namely the gate of 'Hermes and the three Graces'. On the right pillar of the gate, you will see the vague traces of a relief depicting a naked man with a cloak over his shoulder, walking in front of three women. Research has confirmed that these portray Hermes and the three Graces.

Hermes, which was depicted on both gates, was known as the most intelligent of all the Olympian gods and was the messenger to the gods ('Mercury' in Roman mythology); that is why he's wearing winged golden sandals, a winged hat and a magic wand. He is the god of commerce (these gates opened onto the commercial port); he also guides the souls of the dead to the underworld and is the bringer of dreams to mortals.

The three Graces (Euphrosyne - *Joy*, Aglaia - *Beauty* and Thalia - *Good Cheer*) were the favourites of Hermes and the role of these goddesses was to attend to both gods and men during the most agreeable moments in their lives. Their presence was said to guarantee a more beneficial and lasting experience.

Evreocastro and ancient theatre

Continue on what becomes a rough path and you will reach the edge of Evreocastro ('Hebrew Castle'), a beautiful peninsula with a modern chapel that stands on the site of an ancient sanctuary and a later early Christian church of the 5th or 6th century A.D.

At Evreocastro the path turns sharp right (here you will see the remains of one of the towers that was situated on the ancient city wall), ascending at a greater gradient you follow the wall towards the theatre and acropolis, these are some of the best preserved remains of the ancient city wall. I would advise that, especially on hot days, you take water with you on this part of the walk, as from here there is nowhere to obtain refreshment and it takes about an hour. Also those with health problems or disabilities should be aware that the path to the acropolis is steep and uneven.

The theatre is built within the hill's natural bowl, and according to Hippocrates existed from at least the 5th century B.C. The theatre has recently undergone some restoration, so that once again it can be the venue for performances of plays and local events.

The proscenio (forestage) was dedicated to Dionysus in the middle of the 4th century B.C., by the Thassian Lysistratos, son of Kodes. The beginning of the 3rd century B.C. saw the building of the scene (stage) with a marble frontage. At this time, the theatre was used for theatrical and musical performances. Today only one complete pillar and various other sections of the forestage remain. Later in the Roman era, the orchestra pit and the edolia (rows of seats) were renovated. Inscribed names on a number of seats, indicate that the rich and famous could reserve their own space.

After the 1st century A.D., the theatre was also used for animal fights and gladiatorial combats. Among the usual combats, there were also contests between pairs of mounted riders. The orchestra pit was turned into an arena and, in the mid 2nd century A.D., Eragoras, son of Eufrillos, raised a parapet of railings embedded into marble slabs to protect the audience from the wild animals used in the arena. On one of those slabs, you can still see the carved name of a benefactress, Espani, who commanded in her 'last will and testament', that the annual hippodrome festivities in Thessalonika (mainland Greece), be celebrated in her memory.

At this time, the forestage was adorned with reliefs of the highly esteemed ancient gods: Dionysus treating his panther to the last drops of wine from a Kantharus (a vessel with handles, similar to a goblet), the riding hero Hares holding a lance and shield and Heron, a Thracian god, hunting a boar (the former being currently on display in the Museum of Thassos and the latter in the Museum of Constantinople). The Kionostichia (row of pillars) hosted, on its edges, a statue of Nemesis (created at the expense of the gladiator Evimeros, son of Dionysius), as well as other statues, again depicting Nemesis, created at the expense of other unnamed gladiators of that time. Two of these reliefs are also currently on display in the Museum of Constantinople.

In Greek mythology, Nemesis is the goddess of divine justice and vengeance. It is said that her anger is directed toward human transgression, pursuing the wicked with unremitting vengeance. Her cult probably originated from Smyrna (modern day Izmir, Turkey), where she was regarded as the daughter of Zeus and Oceanus.

Most Greek sculpture was of bronze (most of which has sadly been melted down in antiquity). It is worthy of note that today we view ancient marble sculpture as looking magnificent, made of the pure white stone. In antiquity though, these sculptures and many other works of art were painted in realistic colours, covering what we now view as beautiful!

Acropolis and Byzantine castle

From the theatre continue up to the acropolis, following the lampposts. On the first level the acropolis is a long and narrow terrace, which during antiquity was the site of the sanctuary of Pythius Apollo. In Byzantine times the area formed the natural buttress of the town and also acted as a lookout post as its position is 137 metres above sea level. It was at this time that the medieval castle you see today was constructed, a work of Byzantine architects, which was completed during the first half of the 15th century A.D. by the Genoese Gattilusi's dynasty.

When you leave the fortress at the southern end, down the steps and through the archway gate, turn right and you will see on your right a well-preserved late 4th century B.C. funerary stele (gravestone), re-used during the building of the castle defences. It depicts the deceased male lying on a couch in a heroic pose, holding what was likely a wine goblet. A snake, an emblem of the underworld, rears up in front of him. His wife (seated) looks on, whilst behind her is the man's horse (obviously favoured by the man and a sign of his status). Behind the figures, the man's armour (greaves, cuirass [torso armour] and part of the shield [Hoplon]) is portrayed, but would have extended onto the block above. To the far right, a servant stands attentively behind the couch.

The path continues up to the second level of the acropolis, where you will find the ruins of the sanctuary of Athena, with a splendid view over the town and sea. On the final and highest level, is the sanctuary of the god Pan, enclosed within an artificial cave. Although it is the most humble of all the Thassian sanctuaries, it is the one that today's visitor finds especially interesting.

An embossed carving inside the cave portrays the goat-legged god, a loyal follower of Dionysus, nonchalantly resting and playing the Syrinx. The less than artistic quality of the relief does nothing to decrease the graceful portrayal of the subject that dates from around the 4th century B.C.

This completes the tour of group one. Return back down the path, and just before the theatre keep to the left path and you re-enter the town past the Dionysion.

Group two

Southern gates, Heraclion, arch of Caracalla and necropolis

In the following section I have endeavored to present an easy to follow guide to the remaining important archaeological sites in Limenas (I hope you will agree).

On Limenas harbour front, you will find the quay where the Flying Dolphin hydrofoil docks. With your back to the sea, walk across the sea front road and enter the road directly opposite (with a slight 'dog leg'). As you walk up this road you will come to a square on your left, which contains the remains of a Byzantine Basilica, probably dating to the early 6th century A.D.

Continue on and you will come to a junction of five roads, cross the junction and continue up the French Archaeological School Road (Odos Galic Arceolog Scolis). At the end of the houses you arrive at the junction with Devambez Road (Pier De Vambez), directly in front is the 'Heraclion'.

Heraclion

Heracles was the most significant god of Thassos and according to tradition it was the Phoenicians who brought his worship to the island. The Scale and the Propylaea were the monumental entrances to the sanctuary that had a paved path leading to the altar at its centre, only one quadrangle foundation is currently preserved. Here was the point where the people of Thassos gathered on the god's great celebrations called the 'Heraclia', during which military and athletic events and symposiums were held.

The northern part of the site is occupied by the Heraclion temple, which was surrounded by an Ionic colonnade. If you walk over to the information board you can read amongst other information, how in 405 B.C., the Spartan general Lysander, after defeating the Athenian navy at the Battle of Aegospotami (on the coast of Turkey) the previous year, landed on the island, gathered all the Thassian supporters of Athens inside the Heraclion and slaughtered them.

Arch of Caracalla

On the opposite side of Devambez Road and to the right, are located the remains of the triumphal arch of the Roman Emperor Marcus Aurelius Antoninus, better known as Caracalla (Emperor from 211 - 217 A.D.). Dated to the time of his visit to Thrace between 213 and 217 A.D., however, sadly it is poorly preserved.

Necropolis artifacts

Retrace your steps up Devambez Road away from town (with the Heraclion on your left), cross over the intersection with French Archaeological School Road and almost immediately on your right is an area which has been used to store sarcophagi and other monumental pieces from around the island. It is a bit of a jumble, but worth a look around.

Gate of Zeus and Hera

Pass by the necropolis on your right up Devambez Road and in approx. 100 metres you will come to the gate of 'Zeus and Hera', which in antiquity was the main gate into the city. The two main gate pillars had monumental reliefs, one now sadly destroyed, portrayed Zeus and Hera. On the other remaining pillar is the figure of the throned Hera, clad in a pleated Chiton, with Iris her messenger standing infront. Hera was the wife and older sister of Zeus and presided as goddess of marriage, which further emphasised her submission to the patriarchal bond. Her resistance to the many conquests of Zeus is portrayed as 'Hera's jealousy', the main theme of literary anecdotes that underpinned her ancient cult.

On the other side of the road from the gate of Zeus and Hera and slightly to the right (away from town) you will see a dirt track with a broad entrance, opposite the large sarcophagus of Poliades (3rd century A.D.). Walk down this track that runs parallel to the ancient city walls and in approximately 150 metres you should see, dependant on the state of the vegetation, the ruins of a further gate (structurally the largest remaining), that of 'Heracles and Dionysus' (dated to the end of the 4th century B.C.). Opposite seven tall trees there is a rough path that leads through the undergrowth to the gate.

Gate of Heracles and Dionysus

Heracles and Dionysus were the two guardian gods of Thassos (Phylakoi). Heracles was the greatest of the Greek heroes, a paragon of masculinity and champion of the Olympic gods. Dionysus was a notorious consumer of wine (he was the Thracian god of wine) and was said to be invariably drunk and had to be supported by satyrs, or carried on a donkey. In his favour he was also viewed as the promoter of civilization, a lawgiver, and lover of peace, as well as the patron deity of agriculture and the theatre. The original engraving on one gate pillar was removed to the museum in Istanbul, the other was sadly lost in transit. If you walk through the gate you will find on the right inner side of the wall, a flight of steps that originally led up to the battlements.

The wall next to this gate can give you some idea of how spectacular the ancient city would have appeared in antiquity, with glistening white marble walls 5 - 7 metres high, with painted gateways leading to the equally magnificent marble city. Telesicles certainly achieved everything the oracle at Delphi had asked of him. *"Tell the Parians, Telesicles, that I have ordered you to build upon the Isle of Aeria a great city that will be visible from all around."*

Moving on, continue down the dirt track and where it joins the main road (French Archaeological School Road), you will see approx. 30 metres to your left, the gate of 'Silenus'.

Gate of Silenus

Silenus was described as the oldest, wisest and most drunken of the Satyrs, who were the followers of Dionysus. On the left hand pillar of his gate, you will see engraved the figure of Silenus, naked except for a pair of high boots, with erect phallus, long beard and a horse's tail. He seems to be heading to town holding a Kantharus (a large handled goblet) in his right hand.... with his reputation I am sure it held wine! The niche below and in front of the figure, served as an 'altar' for travellers to leave their offerings in his honour.

Continue down French Archaeological School Road towards town and you will once again come to the Heraclion, the end of this tour.

I should confirm that the 'Heraclion', 'Arch of Caracalla', 'necropolis', the gates of 'Zeus and Hera', 'Heracles and Dionysus' and 'Silenus', are all a short distance from each other, so don't be put off, you will find that it is a casual walk not a marathon to visit them all.

Archaeological sites around Thassos

Aliki

If you walk (or take a car) down the hill from the main road, follow the road that goes right behind the beach tavernas. On your left you will come to a wooden covered gateway that leads to the archaeological site. As you walk down the cobbled path through the trees, you will see on your left a massive ancient sarcophagus, now buried, but which was once at ground level. On one side is a substantial Greek inscription. The sarcophagus is dated to the Roman period. This area was the site of the ancient settlement of Aliki from the 7th century B.C. onwards, which was directly connected to the exploitation of the nearby marble quarries.

On the opposite side of the path to the sarcophagus, a few metres into the undergrowth, are the remains of two large ancient kilns, which were used in the manufacture of quicklime. This was an additional product, derived from the local marble on the site.

Continue on towards the eastern beach, here you will find the ruins of an ancient religious sanctuary dating back to the 7th century B.C. The sanctuary we see today consists of two buildings separated by a corridor that ran down to the sea. The south building can be dated to circa. 500 B.C., whilst the north building has two phases, one Ionic dated to 530/525 B.C. and the later Doric remodelling dated to around 470/465 B.C. In the centre of the front halls of both buildings you can see the remains of low sacrificial altars.

During excavations, a statue of a kouros (a young male) was found in the ruins and also inscriptions relating to the worship of the 'Dioskouri'. These were the saviour gods who were patrons of seamen and were associated with the star constellations of Ursa Major and Ursa Minor (the Great and Little Bear), the prime navigational references in antiquity. The two protected bays of Aliki offered safe anchorage for the ships that transported the marble overseas. Inscriptions on the walls and columns of the sanctuary, left by visiting seamen (mainly from the Roman period), praise the gods and ask for safe passage for their ships.

Behind the sanctuary is a cave (gated), which is believed to have been a place of worship to Apollo. In antiquity caves were seen as mystical, having a direct connection with the gods and the underworld. It is therefore possible that this was also one of the reasons for the whole sanctuary's location. A further cave is located higher up on the hill behind the sanctuary. Having a vertical entrance shaft, it is fenced and therefore not accessible.

Climb the hill behind the sanctuary and you will come to the ruins of two early Christian tri-aisled churches (5th century A.D.). They were abandoned around the 7th century A.D. when the marble quarries were closed. Note the many 'grave cuts', both in and outside the church walls. Greece and the surrounding area played a major role in early Christianity through the travels of the Apostles, especially St. Paul (see Philippi, page 64) and the acceptance of Christianity as the official religion of the Roman Empire by Constantine (285 - 337 A.D.) who ruled from Constantinople (modern day Istanbul).

Passing the churches and walking along the cliff-side path, you will come to the ancient marble quarries. Here you will find a number of inlets, where from the 6th century B.C., marble was quarried and used both on the island and exported. Because of its pure white quality, Thassos marble was prized by successive Mediterranean civilisations and incorporated into many of the finest buildings of antiquity, an example being the famous church of Saint Sophia in Istanbul. At the furthest point of the promontory, you will find two interesting information boards, which present a picture of what the quarries were like in ancient times.

If you descend into the quarries and look carefully, you can still see the drill holes into which pegs were inserted to break the blocks away from the bedrock. You can also see the marks (especially on the cliffs) of the picks and chisels that were used to cut and shape the blocks. Some blocks cracked during the quarrying process and have been left in situ. You can imagine the expletives that must have been uttered after so much wasted effort!
On your walk, look out for a very large circular marble block

emerging from the vegetation on the left of the path. This is a column base, which for some reason never left the site. From its size it must have been destined for some magnificent building, maybe the church of Saint Sophia, or a public building in Rome? Further on you will also see in one of the quarries, two columns, one broken and one enormous intact example, the latter just seems to have been abandoned when the quarry closed.

Continue on the cliff path and this will take you round to the west side of the promontory. As you descend down, on your left and below is another cave that has been used since antiquity as a place of worship. Passing the cave you will return to your starting point.

Skala Sotiras

As you enter Skala Sotiras from Limenas (Thassos Town) you will see a church on the right hand side, situated on a platform above the road. The church covers the remains of a fortified early bronze-age settlement, direct evidence that ancient sites are seen as sacred and are reused over time for important buildings.

Early bronze-age settlements are known throughout the Aegean and Asia Minor, dating to between the 4th and 3rd millenniums B.C. As with Skala Sotiras, they are usually small with few buildings within the fortified wall-circuit, the remainder of the settlement extending outside the walls. The fortress walls probably protected a local chief and his entourage, who gained their power from the control of sea trade and rare commodities such as metals.

During the excavations, megalithic stelae representing warriors or hunters were found embedded in the walls of the fortress and examples are now displayed at the back of the excavation as well as in the Museum of Thassos.

Sadly the monument is fenced off and you have to peer through the chain link fence to see the archaeological features. However, as Skala Sotiras is the most important bronze-age site on Thassos, it is worth a visit.

Visiting Kavala

A visit to the mainland and Kavala is a must and is easier than you might expect. There are three ways of getting there, first either by the ferry from Prinos, direct to Kavala taking approx. 1 hr 35 minutes, or the ferry from Limenas to Keramoti (Keramoti is approx. 15 km by bus or taxi from Kavala), this route takes approx. 35 minutes. The final option is by the Flying Dolphin (hydrofoil) from Limenas or Skala Prinos to Kavala (foot passengers only), which takes about 35 minutes (see 'Getting around').

The cost one way for the ferry is between 2.50 and 3.50 euro per person, with the Flying Dolphin costing 7 euro and 3.50 euro for a child each way. The Flying Dolphin has only one return service in the afternoon at 14:00 to Limenas and 12.15 to Skala Prinos. My advice therefore is to take the Flying Dolphin *to* the mainland, so allowing you the maximum time there and *return* by ferry.

Bus services on Thassos are linked to the ferry timetables, so on your return to either port, there should be a bus waiting to take you back to your resort if required.

Kavala (population 63,293) lies in the Gulf of Kavala in the northern Aegean Sea. The town is built on a promontory that stretches south into the gulf and opposite the island of Thassos (13 km distant). Kavala is a modern city with traditional quarters and has a long and complex history. It now plays an important role in the surrounding areas of Macedonia and Thrace. It has the reputation of being the most beautiful city in Macedonia.

The new town spreads out north of the main harbour, which was formed by the construction of two long moles after World War II. The centre offers all the shopping opportunities and services of a modern city, there's even a Marks & Spencer! If you ask for directions to Kapnergati Square, you will find not only the M&S store, but also a good selection of modern fashionable shops and bars.

The Turkish quarter (Panagia) is surrounded by Byzantine walls and occupies the promontory that is crowned by a Byzantine castle. There has been little development of this area, so Panagia keeps its traditional Turkish look, with old and sometimes distinctly rickety houses lining the alleyways.

I certainly believe that a visit to the castle is worthwhile (even if a little tiring in the heat of the day), not necessarily for the castle itself, as there is little to see, but for the beautiful views of the city and the surrounding areas, including a panoramic view of the Gulf of Kavala and the island of Thassos.

As you descend from the castle, you will pass the 'Imaret' that Mehmet Ali (see page 9) built in 1818 as a gift to the people of Kavala. An Imaret was an inn or hostel for Islamic pilgrims and this Imaret has now been restored and converted into a first class hotel (The Imaret Hotel), with luxurious rooms that ooze history and offer fantastic views over the harbour and gulf.

Mehmet Ali's house

Situated in the Seraidaris Garden is 'Kamares', a typical 18th century Turkish designed house and the birthplace of Mehmet Ali, the founder of the last Egyptian royal line. This finely preserved building contains beautiful paneling and carved wooden beams. In the summer months it is a café-bar and during the winter it is a restaurant, opening at 20:00hrs.

Below the house were both the stables and kitchen and on the first floor the Pasha's harem and private quarters. There is a bronze statue of Mehmet Ali Pasha seated on a horse in the small square just beside the building.

The house is not well signposted, but if you continue up the road that the Imaret Hotel is on (a cul-de-sac), just before the end you will come to the square on your left, bordered by a domed church and the house. From here you can also take in some great panoramic views of the bay and city below.

Roman aqueduct

A wide span three-tiered Roman aqueduct dominates the old town. Although worth a visit, it has been heavily restored by subsequent rulers of Kavala. If you take the road that passes under the last arch (the furthest up the hill and away from the town centre), you will find on the other side of the aqueduct and to your left, two old Turkish houses built into the arches, reminiscent of something from 'Eastenders', but a lot more attractive and worth a photograph.

I would also suggest that if you are a little adventurous, you walk up the hill past these houses and after the steepest part of the road you will see on your left, a large white four-storey building. Take the steps just in front of this building that lead up to some ruined outhouses. Just behind these is the top of the aqueduct where you get the best view of its 'snaking' course through the valley below and the capping stones that prevented the water from becoming polluted.

Kavala archaeological museum

A wide range of Roman and Byzantine artifacts have been found in and around Kavala and many of these are now housed in the archaeological museum. So if ancient history is your 'thing', the museum is well worth a visit.

The present Kavala Archaeological Museum opened in 1934 and has occupied its present premises at 17 Erythrou Stavrou Street since 1964. If you walk down the port promenade road from the Flying Dolphin dock, the museum is about 600 metres on your right. It is one of the most important archaeological museum in eastern Macedonia, with prehistoric finds from all over the prefecture of Kavala and from the excavations of Neapolis (the ancient name for Kavala), Amphipolis and other sites within eastern Macedonia.

A number of finds from ancient Amphipolis are displayed on the ground floor: a marble bust of a woman (4th century B.C.), a marble grave stele of an Ephebe (defined as a Greek youth of 18 - 20 years) dated to the 5th century B.C., a large gold finger ring and a gold olive wreath that were found in Macedonian Tomb 1 at Amphipolis (300 B.C.), a headless marble statue of a woman wearing a peplos (1st century B.C.) and a portrait bust of the Roman Empress Agrippina (wife of Emperor Claudius). In the next room are architectural exhibits from the sanctuary of the goddess Parthenos in Neapolis, together with a large collection of ceramics and figurines dated to the archaic period from various workshops including Corinth, Chios and the Cyclades.

On the first floor are antiquities from Galepsos, Oisyme, ancient Topeiros, Abdera, Mesembria, and ancient Tragilos. They include black-figure wares, clay figurines, clay sarcophagi, a painted cist grave, metal pots, and coins of the Macedonian kings. Prime exhibits include a Cycladic amphora (7th century B.C.) and a red-figure hydria (4th century B.C.), which were used as cinerary urns (a vessel containing the ashes of the deceased) and excavated at a cemetery in Oisyme and a poros (a type of stone) sarcophagus with a decorated interior from a sepulchral monument at ancient Tragilos (300 B.C.).

In the courtyard and the atrium there are engraved grave and votive stelae and architectural pieces from various parts of eastern Macedonia, dated to the Roman period.

The museum also holds temporary exhibitions on specific subjects/finds.

Opening times : Summer
Tuesday - Friday : 08:00 - 19:00 (Closed Monday)
Weekends : 08:00 - 14:30

There is a small admission charge of 2 euro per person.

In Eleftherias Square, one city block in from where the fishing boats dock, you will find the Kavala Tourist Information Centre (tel. 2510 231011), where you will be able to obtain city maps and further information on Kavala and any future events.

Visiting Philippi

If your aim is to visit Philippi, there are two main options. The first is to travel there independently by taking the ferry, or better still the Flying Dolphin, from Thassos to Kavala.

Next to the Flying Dolphin dock in Kavala, you will see a multi-storey grey and white building directly in front of you, with signs for the 'Hellenic Coast Guard' and 'Kavala Port Authority' offices. Go down the road on the left hand side of this building (the wide port promenade road), after one city block you will come to a broad road (Mitr Hrissostomou) on your right with buses parked on both sides, this is the main Kavala bus station. Enquire here for the correct bus to Philippi and ask the driver to let you know when you arrive at Philippi. The archaeological site is approx. 19 km from Kavala, takes about 30 minutes and costs around 5 euro per person return. Staff at the site will be able to confirm the bus times for your return to Kavala, which run approx. every half-hour.

Although there is a café on site, I would advise that you take a bottle of water with you, especially in the high season, as the site is extensive with little shade.

The second option is to visit by booking an organised tour to Philippi (these will usually include a trip to the Alistrati Cave in their itinerary), the cost of these tours is around 60 euro per adult. If you have come to Thassos on a package deal, I am sure it will be one of the excursions on the tour company's itinerary. Alternatively there are a number of tour operators in the main towns that offer similar tours at usually a lower cost, so I would advise that you check on prices before booking.

Although for some, an organised tour allows you to relax completely, I myself hate being rushed by tour guides when I am exploring for myself. I therefore prefer to make my own plans and in the many years of travelling, I have found this both more exciting and rewarding. The choice is inevitably yours.

Whichever choice you decide on, you will find that the ticket office has a range of maps and books on the history of the site and its archaeology, which will help enhance the experience.

On site there is a modern air-conditioned lounge, bar, snack facilities and toilets.

I have included a map of the site on page 181.

Summer opening times : Daily: 08:00 –19:30 (Excluding 15th August and 28th October). Adult entrance fee is 3 euro.

A history of Philippi

In the following section I have covered the history of Philippi in detail for those who, like myself, are interested in history and archaeology.

Philippi is famous for a number of historic events, first its close connection with Philip II and his son Alexander the Great. Second for its association with the missionary journeys of the Apostle St. Paul, and last, but by no means least, as the setting for the decisive battle between Mark Antony and Octavian against Brutus and Cassius, the latter two being the main conspirators in the murder of Julius Caesar. It is a sobering thought that if this battle had turned out differently.... and it very nearly did.... Europe and inevitably the World, would be a very different place today.

Origins of Philippi

Philippi lies on the mainland, 17 km northwest of Kavala and was originally founded in circa 360 B.C. by Thassians, led by the exiled Athenian orator Kalistratos. It was however likely, that the colony named Krenides (Greek: Κρηνδες, 'the fountain') by the Thassians, was on the site of a previous settlement. The objective of founding the town was to take control of the neighbouring gold mines and to establish a garrison at this strategic position. Krenides controlled the route between Amphipolis and Neapolis (modern-day Kavala), part of the great royal route that crossed Macedonia from the east to the west, which was later reconstructed by the Romans as the Via Egnatia*.

Its position lies near the head of the Aegean Sea and at the foot of Mount Orbelos (modern-day Mount Lekani). To the south and southwest at that time, there was a marsh that covered the entire plain separating it from the Pangaion hills.

In 356 B.C. the King of Macedonia, Philip II (father of Alexander the Great) conquered Amphipolis and then Krenides, changing its name to Philippi.

Philip II endowed the new city with massive walls and fortifications, which partially blocked the passage between the swamp and Mount Orbelos and sent colonists to occupy it. Philip also had the marsh partially drained, as is attested by the contemporary writer Theophrastus. The discovery of new gold mines near the city, at Asyla, contributed to the wealth of the kingdom and led Philip to establish a mint there. The city was finally fully integrated into the Macedonian kingdom under Philip V. The city remained despite its modest population of perhaps 2,000.

Almost nothing is known about the city in this period. All that remains is the Greek theatre, the foundations of a house under the Roman forum, the walls and a little temple dedicated to a hero cult. This monument covers the tomb of a certain Exekestos and is dedicated to Ktistès, the founding hero of the original city.

The Roman defeat of the Macedonians at the Battle of Pydna in 168 B.C. effectively marked the end of the Antigonid dynasty of Macedonia, which had come to power after the death of Alexander the Great. After their victory, Rome divided Macedonia into four separate states (*merides*), it was Amphipolis and not Philippi that became the capital of the eastern Macedonian state.

Philippi during the Roman era

The city reappears in the sources during the Roman civil war that followed the assassination of Julius Caesar. Caesars heir Octavian and his greatest friend and supporter Mark Antony, confronted the principal conspirators in the assassination, namely Brutus and Cassius, at the Battle of Philippi on the plain to the west of the city in October 42 B.C. Antony and Octavian were victorious in this final battle against the partisans of the Republic. They released some of their veteran soldiers, probably from legion XXVIII, and settled them in the city, which was re-founded as Colonia Victrix Philippensium.

Later he reorganised the colony renaming it Colonia Julius Philippensis and established more settlers there, including both veterans from the Praetorian Guard and other Roman citizens. In 27 B.C., Octavian was given the name Augustus by the Roman senate and was proclaimed Roman Emperor after which the city was once again renamed Colonia Augusta Julius Philippensis.

Following the second renaming, and perhaps after the first, the territory of Philippi was centuriated (divided into squares of land) and distributed to the colonists. The city kept its Macedonian walls, and its general plan was modified only partially by the construction of a forum, a little to the east of the site of the Greek agora. It was organised as a 'miniature Rome,' under the municipal law of Rome and governed by two military officers, the Duumviri, who were appointed directly from Rome.

The colony recognised its dependence on the mines that brought it its privileged position on the Via Egnatia*. Its wealth was demonstrated by the many monuments that were particularly imposing, considering the relatively small size of the urban area. The forum laid out in two terraces on both sides of the main road, was constructed in several phases between the reigns of Emperors Claudius and Antoninus Pius, and the theatre was enlarged and expanded in order to hold Roman games. There is an abundance of Latin inscriptions at the site testifying to the prosperity of the city.

**The Via Egnatia is the name of the Roman road that connected ports on the Adriatic Sea with Byzantium. Although completed in stages, it was begun in around 146 B.C. and expanded and repaired by the Romans in subsequent centuries. It is named after the second century B.C. Roman proconsul of Macedonia, Gnaios Egnatios. Its length varied according to the period, but Roman milestones suggest it was 535 Roman miles long (493 miles).*

St. Paul in Philippi

In 49 or 50 A.D., the Apostle Paul visited the city during his second missionary journey. According to the book of Acts, he was guided there by a vision of 'a man of Macedonia' (Acts 16:9). Accompanied by Silas, Timothy, and probably Luke, Paul preached in Philippi. The Jewish community there seems to have been small, but Paul and his friends found Jewish women gathered at a river to the west of the city on the Sabbath. There Paul baptized Lydia, a purple dye merchant, who invited the missionaries to stay at her home (Acts 16:14 -15).

In another account recorded in Acts, Paul drove out an evil spirit from a slave girl who worked as a fortune-teller. Her owners became angry and dragged Paul and Silas before the city magistrates. A crowd joined in the condemnation, and the apostles were stripped and flogged, before being thrown into prison. At midnight a great earthquake occurred and the prison doors flew open. The jailer, who was so petrified he contemplated suicide, was calmed by Paul who then converted him to Christianity. The next morning the magistrates released Paul and Silas, evicting them from the city (Acts 16:16 - 40). Paul visited the city on two further occasions, in 56 and 57 A.D.

The Epistle to the Philippians dates from around 54 - 55 and shows the immediate impact of Paul's preaching. The subsequent development of Christianity in Philippi is well attested, notably by a letter from the Polycarp of Smyrna addressed to the Christian community in Philippi, dated to around 160, and by funerary inscriptions found at the site.

Philippi during the early Christian era

The first attested church in the city was a small building that was probably originally a prayer house. This Basilica of Paul, confirmed by a mosaic inscription on the pavement, dated to around 343 and from a mention by Bishop Porphyrios, who was present at the Council of Serdica that year (a meeting of the bishops of the early Roman church to agree the laws and future of the church).

Although there is neither archaeological nor literary evidence for the foundation of the Christian community by Paul, the prosperity of the city in the 5th and 6th centuries was attributed to him and to his martyr cult. As in other cities, many new ecclesiastical buildings were constructed at this time. Seven churches were constructed in Philippi between the mid 4th century and the end of the 6th century, some of which competed in size and decoration with the most beautiful buildings in Thessalonica, or even those of Constantinople.

The relationship of the plan and of the architectural decoration of Basilica 'B' with the churches of Saint Sophia and Saint Irene in Constantinople, accorded it a privileged place in the history of early Christian art. The complex cathedral that took the place of the Basilica of Paul at the end of the 5th century was constructed as an octagonal church, which was also said to rival the churches of Constantinople.

In the same period, the fortifications of the city were rebuilt in order to better defend against the growing instability in the Balkans. In 473, the city was besieged by the Ostrogoths, who unable to take it, reaped vengeance on the surrounding villages, burning them to the ground.

Philippi during the Byzantine and Ottoman eras

Already weakened by the Slavic invasions at the end of the 5th century, which ruined the agrarian economy of Macedonia and then by the Plague of Justinian in 547, the city was almost totally destroyed by an earthquake around 619, from which it never recovered. There was a small amount of activity in the late 7th and into the 8th century, but the city was now hardly more than a village.

It is likely the Byzantine Empire maintained a garrison there, but in 838 the city was taken by the Bulgars under Khan Isbul, who celebrated their victory with a monumental inscription on the Stylobate in Basilica 'B', now partially in ruins. The site of Philippi was so strategically important, that in around 850, the Byzantines attempted to recapture it. Several seals of civil servants and other Byzantine officials, dated to the first half of the 9th century, prove the presence of Byzantine armies in the city.

Around 969, Emperor Nicephorus II Phocas rebuilt the fortifications on the acropolis and in part of the city. These gradually helped weaken Bulgar power and strengthen the Byzantine presence in the area. In 1077, further improvements to the city defences were carried out by the Bishop of Philippi, Basil Kartzimopoulos. Philippi began to prosper once more, as witnessed by the Arab geographer Al Idrisi, who mentions that in 1150, it is a centre of business and wine production.

After a brief occupation by the Franks after the Fourth Crusade and the capture of Constantinople in 1204, the city fell into the hands of the Serbs. Still, it remained a notable fortification on the route of the ancient Via Egnatia; in 1354, the pretender to the Byzantine throne, Matthew Cantacuzenus, was captured there by the Serbs.

The city was abandoned at an unknown date. However, when the French traveller Pierre Belon visited Philippi in the 16th century, there was nothing but ruins, with the Turks using it as a quarry. The name of the city was preserved at first by a Turkish village on the nearby plain, Philibedjik, which has since disappeared, and then by a Greek village in the mountains.

Archaeological excavation at Philippi

Only noted or briefly described by 16th century travellers, the first archaeological description of the city was made in 1856 by Perrot, then in 1861 by L. Heuzey and H. Daumet in their famous *Mission Archéologique de Macédoine*. Nevertheless, the first excavations did not begin until the summer of 1914, and were soon interrupted by the First World War.

The excavations, carried out by the École Française d'Athènes, were reinstated in 1920 and continued until 1937. During this time the Greek theatre, the forum, Basilicas 'A' and 'B', the baths, and the walls were excavated. After the Second World War, Greek archaeologists returned to the site.

From 1958 to 1978 the Société Archéologique, then the Service Archéologique and the University of Thessalonica uncovered the bishop's quarter and the octagonal church, large private residences, a new basilica near the museum and two others in the necropolis to the east of the city.

If you visit, you will more than likely see the continuing presence of archaeologists, excavating new areas of the site and helping to unravel its fascinating history.

The battle of Philippi

The Battle of Philippi was the final battle in the 'Wars of the Second Triumvirate' and features in the famous Shakespearean play Julius Caesar, being the backdrop for Acts 4 and 5.

After the murder of Julius Caesar in 44 B.C., the assassins were initially pardoned by the senate on the proviso that the conspiritors in his murder, known as the 'Liberators', would accept that Caesar would not, in death, be declared a tyrant. A further condition imposed by the senate on the two leading conspiritors, Brutus (Marcus Junius Brutus) and Cassius (Gaius Cassius Longinus), was that they both leave Rome for the eastern provinces.

In 43 B.C., Caesar's designated successor Octavian (Gaius Julius Caesar Octavianus) was elected consul by the senate. One of his first acts was to decalre the Liberators 'enemies of the state'. After a power struggle erupted between Mark Antony (Marcus Antonius) and Octavian, Brutus and Cassius saw their opportunity and set about rallying futher troops to the rebublican cause from all the eastern provinces. What they did not count on was that Antony and Octavian would bury their differences and join forces against them. Having control of almost all the Roman army in the west, Antony and Octavian saw their opportunity to finally irradicate the problem of Brutus and Cassius and their republican supporters and so gain full control of the Roman world. And so in 43 B.C., the senate was persuaded to declare war against the forces of Brutus and Cassius, justified as final revenge for the murder of Julius Caesar.

The senate agreed that Mark Antony and Octavian with Marcus Aemilius Lepidus would form the Second Triumvirate (Triumvirate means three joint leaders, see page 84). The Triumvirs decided that Lepidus would stay in Rome to control the senate, while in early 42 B.C., the two main partners of the Triumvirate (Antony and Octavian) set out with their best troops, totalling 28 legions. After ferrying their army across the Adriatic and gaining intelligence that the enemy was somewhere in northern Greece, they sent out a scouting force of 8 legions commanded by Norbanus and Saxa, who after passing the city of Philippi, took a strong defensive position at a narrow mountain pass. Antony was following, while Octavian was delayed at Dyrrachium (modern day Durrës on the Albanian coast) because of ill-health, from which he would suffer throughout the Philippi campaign.

The arrival in the Ionian Sea of the Republican Admiral Ahenobarbus, with a large fleet of 130 ships, resulted in cutting the Triumvirs principal supply route with Italy. The Liberators strategy was not to engage in direct battle, but rather to attain a good defensive position and then use their naval superiority to block the enemies communications and supplies and so wear them down.

The Liberators had spent the previous months plundering Greek cities to swell their war-chest and had gathered in Thrace the Roman legions from the eastern provinces and levies from allies. With their superior forces they were able to outflank Norbanus and Saxa, who had to abandon their defensive position and retreat west of Philippi. Thus, Brutus and Cassius could seize a strong defensive position, holding the high ground along both sides of the Via Egnatia, about 3.5 km west of the city. On the south, their position was anchored to a supposedly impassable marsh, while on the north to impervious hills. They had plenty of time to fortify their position with a rampart and a ditch. Brutus put his camp on the north while Cassius was on the south of the Via Egnatia. Antony arrived shortly afterwards and positioned his army on the south of the Via Egnatia, while Octavian put his legions north of the road.

The battle consisted of two engagements in the plain west of Philippi. The initial battle occurred on 3rd October; Brutus faced Octavian, while Antony's forces confronted those of Cassius. At first, Brutus pushed back Octavian and entered his legions' camp. But to the south, Antony defeated Cassius, and Cassius, hearing a false report of Brutus' failure, commanded his freedman to kill him. Brutus rallied Cassius' remaining troops and both sides ordered their army to retreat to their camps and the battle was essentially a draw, but for Cassius' suicide. The second encounter, on 23rd October, finished off Brutus' forces, and he committed suicide in turn, leaving the Triumvirate in full control of the Roman world and sowing the seeds for the change from republic to empire.

The battle in detail

Opposing forces

The Triumvirs' army included 28 legions (other legions had been left behind). The sources report specifically the name of only one legion (IV legion), but other legions present included the III, VI, VII, VIII, X Equestris, XII, XXVI, XXVIII, XXIX, and XXX, testified to by the fact that their veterans participated in the land settlements after the battle. Appian reports that the Triumvirs' legions were almost at full strength. Furthermore, they had a large allied cavalry force (20,000 horsemen with Antony and 13,000 with Octavian). It is necessary to point out that the name 'Octavian' was never used by his contemporaries: he was simply known as Gaius Julius Caesar Octavianus.

The Liberators' army had 19 legions (8 with Brutus and 9 with Cassius, while another 2 legions were with the fleet). Although only two of the legions were at full strength, the army was reinforced by levies from the eastern allied kingdoms. Appian reports that the army mustered about 80,000 foot-soldiers, with allied cavalry numbering a total of 17,000 horsemen, including 5,000 bowmen mounted in the eastern fashion. This army included the old Caesarian legions present in the east, probably including the XXVII, XXXI, XXXIII XXXVI and XXXVII. The loyalty of these soldiers who were supposed to fight against Caesar's great-nephew and heir, was a delicate issue for the Liberators. However, at least the XXXVI legion consisted of old Pompeian veterans, enrolled in Caesar's army after the battle of Pharsalus (page 84).

With this uncertainty in mind, Cassius endevoured in two ways to reinforce his soldiers' loyalty. First with strong speeches, "Let it give no man any concern that he has been one of Caesar's soldiers. We were not his soldiers then, but our country's." Secondly, with a gift of 1,500 Denari for each legionnaire and 7,500 for each centurion. Although ancient sources do not report the total number of men within the two armies, it seems likely that they had a similar strength, (modern historians put the total at about 100,000 men on each side).

The first battle of Philippi

Antony offered battle several times, but the Liberators were not lured into leaving their defensive position. Thus, Antony tried to secretly outflank the Liberators' position through the marshes in the south. With considerable effort he was able to cut a passage through the marshes, raising a causeway above them. This manoeuvre was finally noticed by Cassius, who tried a counter measure by moving part of his army south into the marshes and making a transverse protective wall, aimed at cutting off Antony's outstretched right wing. This led to an allout battle on 3rd October 42 B.C.

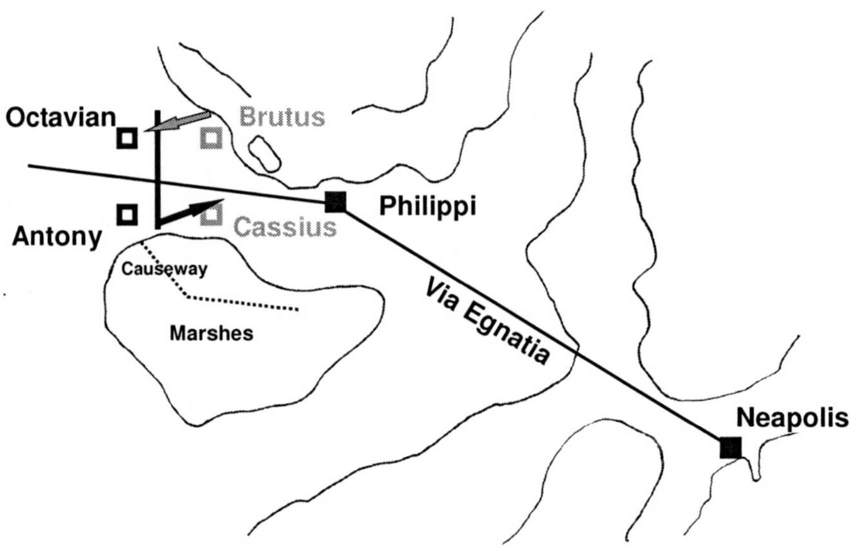

Antony ordered a charge against Cassius, aiming at the fortifications between Cassius' camp and the marshes. At the same time, Brutus' soldiers, provoked by the Triumvirs' army, rushed against that of Octavian, without waiting for the order of attack (given with the watchword 'Liberty'). Luckily this surprise assault achieved complete success, Octavian's troops were put to flight and pursued to their camp, which was captured by Brutus' men, led by Marcus Valerius Messalla Corvinus. Three of

Octavian's legionary standards were also taken, confirming the rout.

Octavian was not found in his tent, his couch was pierced and cut to pieces. Most ancient historians say that he had been warned in a dream to beware of that day, as he himself wrote in his memoirs, Pliny bluntly reports that Octavian went and hid in a marsh. However, on the other side of the Via Egnatia, Antony was able to storm Cassius' fortifications, demolishing the palisade and filling up the ditch. Then he easily took Cassius' camp, which was defended by only a light contingent. It seems that part of Cassius' army had advanced south and when these men tried to return, they were easily repulsed by Antony.

The battle ended in a draw, Cassius had lost 9,000 men, while Octavian had suffered around 18,000 casualties. The battlefield was very large and clouds of dust made it impossible to make a clear assessment of the outcome of the battle, so both parties were ignorant of each other's fate. Cassius moved to the top of a hill, but could still not see clearly what was happening on Brutus' side and believing that his ally had suffered a crushing defeat, Cassius ordered his freedman Pindarus to kill him. Brutus mourned over Cassius' body, calling him "the last of the Romans." However, he avoided a public funeral, fearing its negative effects on the army's morale. As Thassos was one of the main Liberators' bases and provisioning centres, Brutus took the body of Cassius to the island for burial, the site of his grave is unknown.

The second battle

On the same day as the first battle of Philippi, the Republican fleet, patrolling the Ionian Sea was able to intercept and destroy the Triumvirs' reinforcements (two legions and other troops and supplies led by Domitius Calvinus). Thus, the strategic position of Antony and Octavian became quite serious, since the already depleted regions of Macedonia and Thessaly were unable to supply their army for long. Brutus could easily receive supplies from the sea, whereas the Triumvirs had to send a legion south to the Peloponnese to collect more supplies.

The morale of the Triumvirs' troops was boosted by the promise of a further 5,000 Denarii for each soldier and 25,000 for each centurion.

On the opposing side the Liberators' army was left without its best strategic mind. Brutus had less military experience than Cassius and, even worse, he did not command the same level of respect from his soldiers or allies. With this in mind, he offered each soldier a further incentive of 1,000 Denarii.

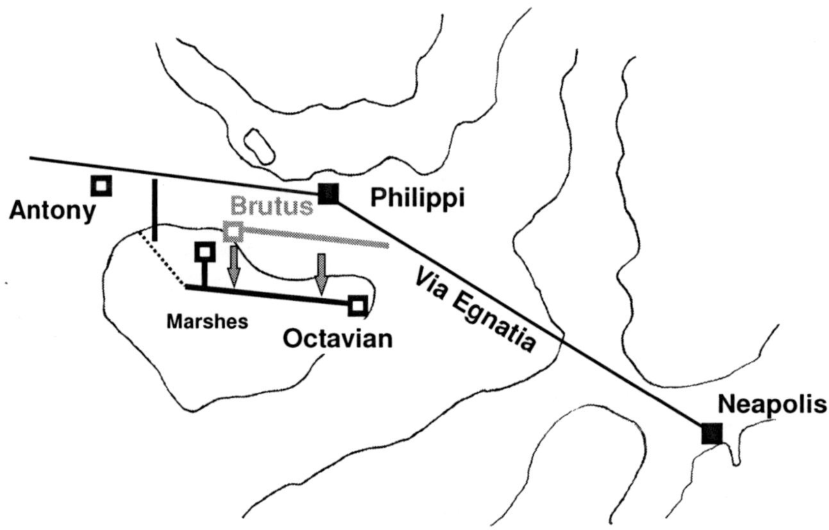

In the next 3 weeks Antony was able to slowly advance his forces south of Brutus' army, fortifying a hill close to Cassius' intial camp site, which had been left unguarded by Brutus.

To avoid being outflanked Brutus was compelled to extend his line to the south, parallel to the Via Egnatia, building several fortified posts. Brutus' defensive position was still secure, holding the high ground with a safe line of communication with the sea and his supply base on Thassos. His aim was to keep to the original plan of avoiding an open engagement and wait for his naval superiority to wear down the enemy.

Unfortunately, most of his officers and soldiers were tired of the delaying tactics and demanded another attempt at an open battle. Probably both Brutus and his officers feared the risk of having their soldiers desert to the enemy, if they did not keep control over their troops. Plutarch also reports that Brutus had not received news of Ahenobarbus' victory in the Ionian Sea.

Thus, when some of the eastern allies and mercenaries did start deserting, Brutus was forced to attack on the afternoon of October 23rd. As he said "I seem to carry on war like Pompey the Great, not so much commanding now, as commanded." The battle resulted in close combat between the two armies of well-trained veterans. Arrows and javelins were largely dispensed with and the soldiers packed into solid shield walls fighting face-to-face with their swords, resulting in a terrible slaughter.

In the end, Brutus' attack was repulsed, and his soldiers routed in confusion, their ranks broken. Octavian's soldiers were able to capture the gates of Brutus' camp before the routed army could reach the safety of this defensive position. Thus, Brutus' army could not reform, making the Triumvirs' victory complete. Brutus was able to retreat into the nearby hills, but with only the equivalent of 4 legions. Seeing that surrender and capture where inevitable, he committed suicide the following day. The total casualties for the second battle of Philippi were not reported, but the close quarter fighting was likely to have resulted in heavy losses on both sides.

Aftermath

Plutarch reports that Antony covered Brutus' body with a purple cloak as a sign of respect and acknowlegdement of their previous friendship and sent his ashes back to Servilia, his mother. He remembered that Brutus had placed a condition on his joining the plot to assassinate Caesar, that the life of Antony should be spared.

Many other young Roman aristocrats lost their life in the battle or committed suicide after the defeat, including the son of the great orator Hortensius, and the son of Cato the younger and Marcus Livius Drusus Claudianus (the father of Livia, who would later become Octavian's wife). Porcia, Brutus' wife, killed herself by swallowing a red-hot coal when she received news of the death of her husband. Some of the senior officers escaped back to their supply base on Thassos, from where they negotiated their surrender to Antony and entered his service. Apparently, they did not want to negotiate with the young and merciless Octavian.

The remains of the Liberators' army were rounded up and roughly 14,000 men were enrolled into the Triumvirs' army. Older veterans were discharged back to Italy, but some of the veterans remained in the city of Philippi, becoming the Roman colony Colonia Victrix Philippensium. Antony remained in the east, while Octavian returned to Italy, with the difficult task of finding suitable land necessary to settle the large number of veterans.

Despite the fact that Sextus Pompeius was still controlling Sicily and Domitius Ahenobarbus continued to command the Republican fleet, the Republican resistance had been irreversibly crushed at Philippi. The Battle of Philippi probably also marked the highest point of Antony's career, at that time he was the most famous Roman general and the senior partner of the Second Triumvirate.

The following eleven years would see the slow but irredeemable breakdown in relations between Antony and Octavian, finally resulting in the Battle of Actium (31 B.C.), when Antony and Cleopatra's forces would be crushed and Octavian would finally gain sole control of the Roman Empire.

Appian of Alexandria (c.95 - c.165 A.D.) is the author of a 'Roman History'. His history of the 'Roman Civil Wars' survives in its entirety. The fourth book contains an excellent account of the double battle of Philippi (translation by Horace White).

On the following day Brutus, seeing the enemy still lying in wait for him, and having fewer than four full legions, which had ascended the mountain with him, thought it best not to address himself to his troops, but to their officers, who were ashamed and repentant of their fault. He sent them to put them to the test and to learn whether they were willing to break through the enemy's lines and regain their own camp, which was still held by their troops who had been left there. These officers, though they had rushed to battle unadvisedly, had been of good courage for the most part, but now, for some divine infatuation was already upon them, gave to their general the undeserved answer that he should look out for himself, that they had tempted fortune many times, and that they would not throw away the last remaining hope of accommodation. Then Brutus said to his friends, "I am no longer useful to my country if such is the temper of these men," and calling Strato, the Epirote, who was one of his friends, gave him the order to stab him. While Strato still urged him to deliberate, Brutus called one of his servants. Then Strato said, "Your friend shall not come short of your servants in executing your last commands, if the decision is actually reached." With these words he thrust his sword into the side of Brutus, who did not shrink or turn away.

So died Cassius and Brutus, two most noble and illustrious Romans, and of incomparable virtue, but for one crime; for although they belonged to the party of Pompey the Great, and had been the enemies, in peace and in war, of Julius Caesar, he made them his friends, and from being friends he was treating them as sons.

The Senate at all times had a peculiar attachment to them, and commiseration for them when they fell into misfortune. On account of those two it granted amnesty to all the assassins, and when they took flight it bestowed governorships on them in order that they should not be exiles; not that it was disregardful of Gaius Caesar or rejoiced at what had happened to him, for it admired his bravery and good fortune, gave him a public funeral at his death, ratified his acts, and had for a long time awarded the magistracies and governorships to his nominees, considering that nothing better could be devised than what he proposed. But its zeal for these two men and its solicitude for them brought it under suspicion of complicity in the assassination, so much were those two held in honour by all. By the most illustrious of the exiles they were more honoured than Sextus Pompeius, although he was nearer and not irreconcilable to the triumvirs, while they were farther away and irreconcilable.

When it became necessary for them to take up arms, it only took less than two years to gather upward of twenty legions of infantry and something like 20,000 cavalry, and 200 ships of war, with corresponding apparatus and a vast amount of money, some of it from willing and some from unwilling contributors. They carried on wars with many peoples and with cities and with men of the adverse faction successfully. They brought under their sway all the nations from Macedonia to the Euphrates. Those whom they had fought against they had brought into alliance with them and had found them most faithful. They had had the services of the independent kings and princes, and in some small measure even of the Parthians, who were enemies of the Romans; but they did not wait for them to come and take part in the decisive battle, lest this barbarous and hostile race should become accustomed to encounters with the Romans.

Most extraordinary of all was the fact that the greater part of their army had been the soldiers of Gaius Caesar and wonderfully attached to him, yet they were won over by the very murderers of Caesar and followed them more faithfully against Caesar's son than they had followed Antony, who was Caesar's companion in arms and colleague; for not one of them deserted Brutus and Cassius even when they were vanquished while some of them had abandoned Antony at Brundusium before the war began. The reason for their service, both previously under Pompey and now under Brutus and Cassius, was not for their own interest, but for the cause of democracy. Both of the leaders, when they thought they could no longer be useful to their country, despised their own lives. In that which related to their cares and labours Cassius gave his attention strictly to war, like a gladiator to his antagonist. Brutus, wherever he might be, wanted to see and hear everything, having been a philosopher of no mean note.

Against all these virtues and merits must be set down the crime against Caesar, which was not an ordinary or a small one, for it was committed unexpectedly against a friend, ungratefully against a benefactor who had spared them in war, and nefariously against the head of the state, in the senate-house, against a pontiff clothed in his sacred vestments, against a ruler without equal, who was most serviceable above all other men to Rome and to its empire. For these reasons heaven was incensed against them and often forewarned them of their doom.

When Cassius was performing a lustration for his army his lictor placed his garland upon him wrong side up; a Victory, a gilded offering of Cassius, fell down. Many birds hovered over his camp, but uttered no sound and swarms of bees settled upon it.

Once when Brutus was about to cross from Asia to Europe with his army, and while he was awake at night and the light was burning low, he beheld an apparition of extraordinary form standing by him, and when he boldly asked who of men or gods it might be, the spectre answered, "I am thy evil genius, Brutus. I shall appear to thee again at Philippi." And it is said that it did appear to him before the last battle.

When the soldiers were going out to the fight, an Ethiopian met them in front of the gates, and as they considered this a bad omen they immediately cut him to pieces. It was due, too, to something more than human, no doubt, that Cassius gave way to despair without reason after a drawn battle, and that Brutus was forced from his policy of wise delay to an engagement with men who were pressed by hunger, while he himself had supplies in abundance and the command of the sea, so that his calamity proceeded rather from his own troops than from the enemy. Although they had participated in many engagements, they never received any hurt in battle, but both became the slayers of themselves, as they had been of Caesar. Such was the punishment that overtook Cassius and Brutus.

For those who are interested in how the historical events discussed in this book sit within the broader Greek, Roman and European history, I have included the following timelines. Those in bold are mentioned in the book.

Greek timeline

Date	Event
776 B.C.	First Olympic Games
circa 750	The start of early Greek culture. Homer creates the epics the 'Iliad' and the 'Odyssey'
680-580	Corinth is ruled by the tyrant Kypselos and then his son Periander
508	Athens becomes a democratic state
490	**Athenians defeat the Persians at the Battle of Marathon**
480	**The 300 Spartans take on the Persians at Thermopylae and are annihilated. Athens defeat the Persian fleet at the Battle of Salamis**
449	**The Treaty of Callias brings peace with Persia**
472-410	Athens flourishes. Most of the famous Greek plays are written during this period
462-429	Perikles is General of the Greek army and is revered as a great leader
432	The Parthenon on the Acropolis in Athens is completed
431-404	The Peloponnesian Wars between Athens and Sparta
404	**Sparta defeats Athens**
338	**King Philip of Macedonia conquers Greece**
336	King Philip is murdered, most likely by his wife and son Alexander. Alexander becomes King
336-323	Alexander the Great, conquers most of the known world, as far as India
146	**Rome conquers Greece and subjugates it**

Early Roman timeline

Date	Event
509 B.C.	Traditionally the year the Roman Republic was founded
396	Romans capture Estruscan city of Veii
390	Rome is sacked by Gauls after its army is slaughtered at the river Allia
275	The Pharos lighthouse at Alexandria is finished
264-241	First Punic War (between Rome and Carthage)
218-201	Second Punic War
216	At Cannae, Rome suffers its worst defeat to the Carthaginian Hannibal
202	Hannibal is decisively defeated at Zama
200-196	Second Macedonian War
192-188	War with Antiochus III
171-167	Third Macedonian War
149-146	Third Punic War
146	City of Carthage is destroyed
133	Tiberius Gracchus introduces novel reforms including land grants to the poor and food distribution; he is murdered
123	Gaius Gracchus, brother of Tiberius is also murdered after initiating reforms along the same lines
107	Gaius Marius is elected consul; begins major reforms of army
88	Rome grants citizenship to all free adult males in Italy

82	Sulla becomes dictator
77	Senate chooses Pompey to put down Sertorius' rebellious army in Spain
73	Uprising of slaves led by Spartacus
71	Crassus and Pompey defeat Spartacus
60	**Pompey, Crassus and Caesar form the First Triumvirate**
59	Caesar elected consul
58-51	Gallic Wars: conquest of Gaul by Julius Caesar
53	Crassus dies at the Battle of Carrhae
49	Caesar defeats Pompey at Ilerda in Spain. Caesar crosses Rubicon river; initiating civil war
48	**Battle of Pharsalus, Caesar defeats Pompey**
46	Caesar becomes dictator
44	**Brutus, Cassius and other senators assassinate Caesar**
43	**Octavian, Antony, and Lepidus form Second Triumvirate**
42	**Antony and Octavian defeat Brutus and Cassius at the Battle of Philippi; destruction of the last republican army**
40	The Roman Senate makes Herod the Great King of Judea
33	**Civil war between forces of Octavian and Antony**
31	**Octavian crushes the naval fleet of Antony and Cleopatra at the Battle of Actium**
27	**Octavian takes the title of Imperator Caesar Augustus; the Empire begins**

Imperial Rome timeline

Date	Event
27 B.C.-14 A.D.	Reign of Augustus as Emperor
9 A.D.	Three Roman legions annihilated by Germanic tribes at the Battle of the Teutoburg Forest
14-37	Reign of Tiberius
37-41	Reign of Caligula
41	The mad Emperor Caligula is stabbed to death
41-54	Reign of Claudius
43	Claudius orders the invasion of Britain
49/50	**St. Paul first visits Philippi**
54-68	Reign of Nero
60-61	Revolt of Boudicca, Queen of the Iceni
64	Great fire in Rome, resulting in the persecution of the Christians
66	Beginning of the Jewish revolt
69	'The Year of The Four Emperors'
69-79	**Reign of Vespasian**
70	The city of Jerusalem is virtually wiped out by Titus
79-81	Reign of Titus
79	Eruption of Mt. Vesuvius; the two cities of Pompeii and Herculaneum are buried in ash
80	Colosseum (Flavian Amphitheatre) opens
81-96	Reign of Domitian
85	Agricola's campaigns in Britain end

98-117	Reign of Trajan
101-106	Trajan conquers Dacia. Arabia is annexed
112-113	Trajan's Forum and Column dedicated
115-117	Jewish revolt
132-135	Bar Cochba's revolt; final diaspora of the Jews. Handrian's villa built at Tivoli. Hadrian's Wall built in Britain
142	Wall of Antoninus Pius built north of Hadrian's Wall
165-167	Rome suffers from severe plague
162-178	Marcus Aurelius campaigns in Germanic Wars (played by Richard Harris in the film 'Gladiator')
180-192	The son of Marcus Aurelius, the egotistical Commodus is Emperor. 192 his wife arranges his murder by strangulation whilst he bathes
208-211	Severus campaigns in Britain. Arch of Septimius Severus erected
211-217	**Caracalla is Roman Emperor**
284-305	Diocletian's Reign
306-337	**Constantine's Reign**
312	The Emperor Constantine converts to Christianity. The Edict of Milan grants legal rights to Christians
325	The Council of Nicea - held to agree the future of the Christian Church
330	Constantine declares Constantinople capital of a Christian Empire
379-395	Reign of Theodosius
378	Battle of Adrianople, eastern Emperor Valens is killed

395	Death of Theodosius I, final division into an Eastern and Western Roman Empire
396-398	The Visigoths ravage Greece
410	Rome is sacked by the Visigoths
418	Visigoths settle in Aquitaine with capital at Toulouse
429	Vandals cross from Spain to Africa
436	Last Roman troops leave Britain
441	The Huns defeat the Romans at Naissus
circa 450	Beginning of Anglo-Saxon settlements in Britain
451	Aetius defeats Attila at the Catalaunian Plain
453	Council of Chalcedon: Constantinople wins ecclesiastical supremacy over Alexandria
455	Vandals sack Rome
476	Romulus Augustulus - last emperor of the west is forced from his throne by the Germanic chieftain Odoacer, who is proclaimed King of Italy
532-537	Justinian builds the Church of Saint Sophia
533-534	Re-conquest of north Africa from the Vandals
535-555	Re-conquest of Italy from the Goths
541-542	Great Plague of Justinian
548	Death of the Empress Theodora
568	Lombards invade Italy
681	The First Bulgarian Empire is formed
690's	Muslims conquer Byzantine north Africa
717-718	Muslims lay siege to Constantinople
1453	**Fall of Byzantine Empire when Turks capture Constantinople**

Visiting the Alistrati Cave

The Alistrati Cave is to be found on the road between Drama and Serres about 65 km northwest of Kavala. The cave is home to a large flock of wild pigeons and it was their presence, flying in and out, that alerted hunters to its existence. However, the cave was not explored until the Commune of Alistrati notified the Hellenic Speleologic (caving) Organization. This was in the spring of 1975, and in September of the same year, a group of professional Greek cavers was sent to explore the system for the first time. In the following month a second team, with members from Austria, made a further study of the cave.

The cave is famous for its beautiful formations of stalagmites, stalactites, curtains, draperies, rim stone pools and soda straws. It is entered today through an artificial tunnel, with the tour path following the main passage, which is wide and high for most of the way and extends for 2,000 metres into the mountainside. About 10 metres down the passage, the pillars stand in rows, with not only the walls but also the stalactites and stalagmites, covered with a thick layer of aragonite crystals.

Most of the side passages are closed to the public to protect the fragile fauna of the cave. Biological examination of the cave brought a wealth of specialised troglodytic animals. The fauna of the cave is extremely rich in the number of species found there. All in all, 44 species were found in the cave, 13 vertebrates and 31 invertebrates. The most famous species is the endemic Alistratia Beroni, a very small insect found only in this cave. One reason for so many troglobionts, is the existence of the bats, which bring a constant flow of food into the cave.

Photography is forbidden, the explanation being to protect the eco-system. This rule is strictly adhered to and you are not even allowed to take cameras into the cave. To compensate, the ticket office staff are helpful and you can safely leave your cameras there for free.

The cave complex although well worth a visit, is quite touristy, with a huge parking lot, a self-service restaurant and a corral to control the visitors queuing for tickets. However, the tours are very professional and are conducted by official multi-lingual guides. The path is absolutely flat, not a single step, and so the whole tour is wheelchair accessible.

In the nearby Aggitis river gorge there are many caves, which since archaic times have been used as shelters. Ancient paintings found in the caverns of the gorge date back to around the 5th century. At present the gorge is only used for white water rafting, although the council of Alistrati plans to build paths and viewpoints into the gorge to make it accessible to visitors.

Entry cost: 3 euro per person.

The cave is open every day and is well signposted from all directions. The temperature in the cave is approx. 20° C.

Opening times:-

During the summer	: 09:00 - 19:00
During the winter	: 09:00 - 17:00

There are three main ways of visiting the cave, first through an organised tour, Alistrati is usually included on the tour of Philippi and this will be found either through your tour operator (if you have one), or through the independent tour operators on the island.

The second is by car, if you do hire a car (and advise the hire company that you are visiting the mainland), you can drive there as well as Philippi, with the journey direct to the cave taking around an hour.

The third is by bus from Kavala via Drama, I have not yet taken this alternative, but will do so during 2008 so that I can personally report on the journey. However, past experience of Greek public transport makes me believe it will be relatively easy and very cost effective.

Beaches and resorts

As with most Greek islands the main beaches are clean, with a gradual gradient into the sea (I have mentioned those that have a steeper gradient) and most are well served by tavernas, bars and shops. The following guide to major beaches starts at Thassos Town and circles the island clockwise, but remember, down most seaward tracks off the island's main road, is a cove or beach (too numerous to mention them all).......but be warned, some of the tracks are very potholed, so be careful when exploring.

If you have young children, just be a little careful on the beaches, as the currents can dredge out small pockets of sand under the water. This can be a shock to a child who finds that one minute they are in water a foot deep and the next up to their necks.

Thassos Town

Thassos Town being the capital of the island is the liveliest resort, with a wide range of bars, restaurants, shops and services. If you walk past the old harbour (past a large multi-chimney two-storey building on your right) you will come to a small beach, well served by tavernas and bars.

Makryammos

Two kilometres to the south of the town lies Makryammos Beach, this beautiful long sandy beach (approx. 250 metres) is surrounded by a thick forest and verdant vegetation. It is one of the most attractive beaches in the area, offering shallow crystalline waters and a fine sandy beach that extends around the bay, perfect for families with young children. However, there may be a small fee to pay at the entrance to the beach.

The Makryammos Resort Hotel (bungalow style accommodation), dominates the area behind the beach and offers some amenities to non-residents.

Golden Beach

The resort certainly lives up to its name with glorious golden sands.

There are a number of quality tavernas and bars at the back of the beach and sun-bed and parasol hire is available along its length. The beach extends into the sea at a very shallow gradient, so you are able to walk out a hundred yards and still be in water up to your waist.

There are two supermarkets on the main street as well as a kiosk for cigarettes, sweets, newspapers etc. The local bus service runs directly into the resort and there is a boat service from Thassos Town. A taxi rank is situated on the main resort road, or you can ask in one of the supermarkets and they will usually be happy to phone for a taxi. All the items you will require for the beach can be purchased at the local supermarkets, including lilos (5 - 15 euro) and parasols (10 - 15 euro). You will find that the supermarkets tend to stay open all day and evening during the summer season.

In rare years, some beaches such as Golden Beach and Skala Potamias can suffer from a mini-plaque of wasps, but all in all, the beautiful setting of the beach makes up for any inconvenience they may cause.

Golden Beach extends along to and merges with Skala Potamias. Paragliding, banana boats, jet skis, windsurfing and canoe/pedalo hire is available along the length of the combined beaches. There is also a water taxi service from Thassos Town to Golden Beach.

Skala Potamias

At the other end of Potamia Bay from Golden Beach is Skala Potamias, which is a more lively and touristy resort. There are a wide range of tavernas just off the beach area and a range of bars serving drinks and snacks. The resort has a disco at night and buzzes with life in the high season. There are numerous supermarkets selling a full range of products and foods. In one of the bars opposite the beach is an internet café, so you can send that quick message home (1 hour costs about 3 euro).

Kinira

Continue south on the main coastal road and you come to Kinira, a small resort with hotels, tavernas and accommodation to let. Many of the tavernas offer a good selection of fresh fish, as this is a main fishing area on the island. At Kinira there is a long beach with fine sand.

Paradise Beach

The first thing I have to say is that part of the beach is reserved for nudist bathing, so if this is not 'your cup of tea', or you are a family, this *may* not be the beach for you!

As its name implies, this beach is considered as one the best beaches on Thassos, reminiscent of a tropical paradise. It is 500 metres long and has fine white sand and shallow clear azure waters. Forested mountains and lush vegetation surround the beach. A number of bars and a little seafood taverna are located directly on the beach. Opposite the beach is the small island of Kinira. When the weather is windy, its topography makes Paradise Beach ideal for windsurfing.

The more adventurous, who venture further on foot, will find sheer cliffs and some fabulous deserted coves at the southern end. Some shade can also be found here from the scorching midday and afternoon sun.

The beach is reached via a narrow track through a small wood near the village of Kinira. Please be aware that the track is very steep and rocky and therefore not really accessible to vehicles other than 4WD's with high ground clearance. The beach is well signposted, but you will also see lots of parked cars at the entrance to the beach on the main road.

Aliki

A beautiful setting for a beach, situated on a promontory jutting out into the sea, however, it does suffer from its own success. In the high season it can become very crowded with coach loads of sun-worshipers arriving throughout the day. Car parking is restricted and confused and inevitably with all of this, it can be a little difficult at times to find a space on the beach. There are five tavernas on the beach serving drinks, light meals, snacks etc. and one 'The Koala Cafe' has the feel of an 'ex-hippy' past, friendly and laid back.

On the opposite side of the peninsula from the main beach, there are the ruins of an ancient Greek sanctuary. If you climb the hill behind the sanctuary, you will come to the ruins of two early Christian churches. Passing these and walking towards the edge of the promontory, you will come to the ancient marble quarries, where you can still see not only the blocks of marble that cracked during quarrying and were left, but also the marks of the drills and picks they used to cut and shape the stone (see page 55).

Astris

Marble slabs slope down to the medium sized beach from the roadside car park at the small but beautiful resort of Astris. A semi-circle of golden sand dips steeply into the sea with two tavernas, one behind the sands and another on top of a nearby hill, completing the scene. The steep beach can create large waves and strong underwater currents, so it is not ideal for families with young children.

Psili Ammos beach

Psili Ammos (means 'fine sand'), lying just north of the village of Astris, is about 250 metres long. It is one of the most striking beaches on the island, because of the fine white sand. The beach inclines gradually and the sea is shallow.

Facilities on the beach include water-skiing, paragliding, and surfing. There are three tavernas and a supermarket nearby.

Potos

On the southwest of the island is Potos a small but attractive, resort. There is a small shopping area (about 50 shops) along one street behind the fishing harbour, with a long curving beach and promenade.

There are about 15 tavernas/bars, mostly in the centre including an internet café, with a terraced row of bars on the beach.

The beach at Potos is sandy and interrupted to the north of the harbour by a dry riverbed. The beach is just to one side of the shopping area, and is about 1,000 metres long. There are sunbeds and parasols, and there are small boats for hire on the beach. The beach has a steep incline into the sea.

Alexandra Beach and Alexandra Beach Spa Resort

The nearby Alexandra beach is a sandy/pebble beach. It is about 400 metres long. Once again there are sunbeds and parasols for hire. There is a beach-bar/taverna, volleyball net, showers and a changing cubicle. The beach has a steeper incline into the sea.

Pefkari

A gently shelving beach and shallow water make this an ideal spot for families with children and the nearby headland offers enjoyable cliff-side walks. There are a number of tavernas and a range of water sports that include surfboards, pedalos, banana boats, paragliding and jet skis. A nearby hotel complex can result in the place becoming rather busy though in the high season. Also keep an eye out for sea urchins; they *can* be a problem here.

Metallia

Just before Limenaria there is a side road on your left that leads down to the small but beautiful beach of Metallia. Here you will find the ruins of an iron processing plant, opened in the early part of the 20th century by the German mining company Speidel and which operated until 1960. Above and behind the beach is the house called 'Palataki' (little palace) that functioned as the company offices. An interesting fact is that during the First World War, Greece although initially neutral had some political factions that were pro-German. One of the concessions to the Germans was to allow them to base Zeppelin airships on Thassos.

I would recommend a visit to Metallia, if nothing more than for the intriguing ruins of the mine workings, which children would especially find fascinating (but parents beware, there are a number of unfenced precipitous drops, both in and outside of the ruins). Above the sandy beach on the terraces is an art exhibition that includes white pebble art, marble sculptures and a maze. Tucked away on the right of the beach is a tunnel hewn out of the rock, which leads through to Limenaria.

Metallia can also be reached by driving into Limenaria, along the promenade road and continue up the hill out of town. As you pass under the high pedestrian iron bridge, there is a road on the right. At the junction there is a small blue sign with a foot, Pefkari and Potos painted on it. Go up this road, which you will find leads to the Palataki car park, from where you can walk through the iron workings down to the beach.

Limenaria

Limenaria is the second largest town on the island having a population of approx. 3,500. There is a fishing harbour and a long waterfront promenade lined with a number of tavernas and bars that front the main town centre. Behind this you can find many old mansion style houses lining small steep streets. These were mostly built in the early 1900's by the Turks, for the management of the German mines nearby. In the main town there is a wide range of shops, restaurants, cocktail bars and an internet café in the centre. There are two outdoor discos on the main road to Potos and a small folklore museum near the centre.

Limenaria has three main and a number of smaller beaches. The main beach (named after the resort) is a very long sandy beach approx. 2,000 metres in length with some pebbles and rocks.

On a clear day, looking out to sea, the peninsula and mountains of Athos, part of Halkidiki are clearly visible.

Trypiti Beach

Trypiti beach, a little west of Limenaria is about 500 metres long, sandy with some pebbles and gravel. There are sunbeds and umbrellas, a small beach bar and two tavernas. The beach inclines steeply into the sea and therefore not ideal for families with young children.

The centre of the beach is sandy with pebbles, rocks and gravel. It is about 100 metres long and has a pier jutting out into sea.

Skala Maries (Marion)

Skala Maries is a lovely little village with a maze of streets and quaint buildings. There is a small beach at the end of the harbour inlet and a promenade along the harbour wall, both well serviced by tavernas.

Skala Kallirachi

The next village along the coast is Skala Kallirachi, which has a small modern harbour, a wide promenade with tavernas extending along the waterfront. There is a very small beach next to the harbour. Below what looks like a ‘mini volcano’ on the mountain behind Skala Kallirachi is the village of Kallirachi with the church of Agio Metamorphis under which is an underground lake.

Skala Sotiras

The resort of Skala Sotiras is located about 3 kilometres south of Skala Prinos, on the western coast of the island. A peaceful beach with fine sand and shallow waters extends in front of the village.

From here you can rent small boats, to explore the local coastline.

Skala Prinos

Skala Prinos has the second largest harbour on Thassos, with ferries leaving here for Kavala. Because of the ferries, there is a good bus service to all parts of the island with the timetable linked to their arrivals and departures. Next to the ferry port is a working shipyard.

From Skala Prinos you have a view of one of the only two oil-drilling platforms in the Aegean-sea. Although they are not the most attractive of structures, most tourists are intrigued and take photos of these steel monsters.

On Mondays, there is a market in the village of Prinos situated above Skala Prinos in the mountains. Megalo and Mikro Kazavitis are two picturesque villages above Prinos, which if you are mobile and have an hour to spare, are worth a visit.

Skala Prinos has two long sandy beaches. One on the left and one on the right of the ferry harbour, but the surrounding area make these less than attractive....unless of course you are a 'Ferry Spotter'!

Skala Rachoni

Skala Rachoni has a large man made harbour, but I am afraid I am not impressed by the area or facilities, however, if you decide to visit, I would appreciate your views for future revisions of the book.

The nearby small Glifoneri beach is sandy and situated in a little bay with rocks on both sides. There are sunbeds and behind the beach are a shower, toilets and a taverna with a terrace.

The Pachis beach (50 metres) is sandy with pebbles and includes a wooden pier stretching out to sea. There are sunbeds and parasols, a shower and two tavernas, both with terraces.

Organised trips

Most tour companies will offer a range of excursions to their customers at the traditional 'welcome meeting'. These range from the sometimes-abused title of a 'Greek Night', day boat trips around the island including a barbeque, spa days, to more exotic options such as a two day trip to Istanbul.

Many of the excursions can also be found independently, through the many tour companies situated in the towns on the island. Whilst the choice is down to the individual, before booking with your tour operator, I would recommend you shop around to see what offers are available and if possible talk to other holidaymakers who have already been on the tour in question.

The cost especially for a family can be considerable, for example, a one day tour of Philippi and the Alistrati Cave with one of the major holiday companies for a family of 4, with the two children under 12, will cost around 200 euro (approx. £140) and this does not include food and beverages.

Whilst I am not decrying organised tours, as some are very good, a little time looking around and asking questions can help you make the most of that hard earned cash.

Activities for the younger visitor

If you have booked hotel accommodation through a tour company, most offer activities for the very young within the hotel precincts, these should be listed in the company's brochure.

Other than the obvious days on the beach, I will outline a range of activities that are suitable for children.

In or near most of the main resorts you can usually find a limited number of fairground attractions for an evening treat (e.g. in Thassos Town, opposite 'Cheers' bar and in Skala Potamias, near the old harbour). These include dodgem rides, mini-carousels and a road-train that takes you around the town.

Boat trips around the island can be booked in most resorts, as can pedalo hire, banana rides and paragliding. The horse riding stables on the island also offer pony rides for the young, both of these are described in more detail later in the chapter on 'Sports and recreation'.

Most of the larger supermarkets and souvenir shops stock a wide range of toys, including such things as children's fishing kits, snorkelling sets and fun beach items, such as bucket and spades, lilos, toy dinghies, frisbees, beach balls, racket ball sets, etc.

The internet cafés on the island tend to attract the younger user and it may be an idea for them to bring any favourite computer game software with them, although most have games already loaded.

For the older teenager, there are two discos in Thassos Town, however, for this age group there is a more limited range of organised activities on Thassos.

All the usual UK battery sizes are available in the supermarkets, but make sure the kids bring the battery chargers for their games consoles and equipment or suffer the consequences!

Getting around

For those who want the convenience, hiring a car is easy on Thassos and the driving conditions are good. As there is only one major road circling the island (98 km), it is difficult to get lost and all the best beaches and villages are simple to find. If you are on the island for more than one week, it may be worth hiring a car for only some of your stay, as the local bus service is reliable, air-conditioned and regular (I have included the bus routes and information in the next chapter). Obviously this is dependant on where you are staying and how accessible your hotel/apartment is to the local bus services. Most of the supermarkets on the bus routes sell tickets and will confirm the bus times. To give you an idea of cost, a single journey from Golden Beach to Thassos Town will cost 1.70 euro per person.

There is also a quality taxi service on the island and to give you an idea of the cost, a late evening taxi (the buses stop running in the evening) from Thassos Town to Golden Beach will cost around 12 euro. Although the taxi companies are very honest, it is always advisable to confirm the price of the journey before starting.

If you decide to hire a car and you are travelling with a tour company, I am sure they will offer to arrange a hire car for you. Alternatively, there is a wide-range of car hire companies on the island and my experience is that they are all of high quality and open to *a little negotiation*, especially at the beginning and end of the season. You can budget on paying around 175 euro for one week's hire of, for example, a Daewoo Matiz or equivalent, which includes air conditioning (a must especially in the high season) and power steering, with prices increasing to around 300 euro for the top end specification of a jeep. However, take account of the fact that although a jeep is seen as more of a fun vehicle and will go where the lower slung 2WD cars won't, it is open to the sun (nice at first, but you can return home looking like a lobster!) and there is usually nowhere to lock up those valuables.

I am not being condescending, but remember to bring your driving licence with you, an obvious thing you may say, but you would be surprised how often people forget and can't hire a car.

With most car hire companies, you can if you wish, take the car onto the mainland via the ferry (you need to advise them of your intention) and although this makes visiting the sites of interest such as Kavala, Philippi and the Alistrati Cave easy and less expensive than the official tours, the traffic is much heavier on the mainland and the rules and regulations are enforced more stringently than back on Thassos. If you park illegally, the police will remove your registration plate and you will have to go and collect it from the police station, as well as of course, pay the appropriate fine.

If you are a little more adventurous, there is always the alternative of taking to public transport on the mainland. The ferry costs between 2 - 2.50 euro per person one-way, with the Flying Dolphin hydrofoil costing 7 euro per adult. Once there, the bus services are equally as cheap and reliable as those back on the island.

On Thassos please be careful when parking in the villages, the roads are very narrow and the local buses weave their way through, with usually inches to spare between the bus and the houses. You will therefore be in trouble if you block the road.

Seat belts are compulsory and 'drinking and driving' is a serious offence with harsh penalties, whether you are on two wheels or four. Police roadblocks for breath-tests, are a regular occurrence, especially in the summer months.

I would also recommend that you take note of the advice of the car company as to which roads your particular vehicle is appropriate for. Many of the un-metalled interior roads look fine as you enter them, but they usually get progressively worse, with large potholes and sometimes with nowhere to turn around. If you don't hire a 4WD take care, or you may find yourself facing a hefty bill for any resulting damage to the car.

One important piece of advice is that if you are unfortunate and have an accident, stay where you are, calm down and phone the car hire company. Do not leave the scene of the accident, as this can invalidate your insurance and you can be left paying for the full cost of the damage.

Fuel is readily available with modern service stations throughout the island. Prices are on average just above the 1 euro a litre and that includes the personal service of an attendant filling the tank.

The one thing that will amaze the visitor is the lack of traffic. At certain times of day you can drive for kilometres without seeing another vehicle......one of the many 'pluses' of being an ex-pat on Thassos. One statement to amuse your passengers is as the one car in ages passes by; you can declare, "it must be rush hour!"

Last of all, if you return the car late, or in a dirty condition, the hire company may impose a further charge.

Scooter and motorbike hire

Now we come to the hire of the two-wheel mode of transport. Although initially very attractive, especially to the younger visitor, as the cost is low and there are many hire companies promoting them, I have seen so many serious accidents involving motorbikes or scooters in Greece, that I would recommend anyone young or old, to think again and if they can afford it, indulge themselves in the extra cost of a car.

Although all the hire companies supply crash helmets, most people you see on two wheels, are dressed in shorts and T-shirts and I have seen the result of flesh contacting tarmac and gravel. Even at low speeds, the resulting injuries are enough to put anyone off the idea for life!

With regard to pedal cycles, I will include them in more detail in the chapter on 'Sports and recreation'. I have noticed a surprising number of visitors using this form of transport, but there are a lot of hills on Thassos and as I am a person who prefers a motor in front of me, I cannot quite understand the attraction, especially when you are supposed to be on holiday. For those that can, I have included information on cycle hire later.

Bus information

In the 2006 and 2007 editions of this book, I included the complete bus timetables. However, the constant changes made by the bus company, meant that they were more often out of date than accurate.

I have therefore made the decision that in this and future editions, I will only include the routes, a guide to costs and a little extra useful information.

When you arrive you can obtain a copy of the timetables from most supermarkets, or the bus company offices on the main promenade road in Thassos Town.

When using the buses, it is advisable wherever possible to buy your tickets from the local supermarket, as the bus drivers will be reluctant to accept payment on-board if tickets are available near to the pick-up point.

Food and drink are not allowed to be consumed on-board the buses and you should wear a top when travelling (the reason being to stop those sweaty and oil covered bodies soiling the seats).

On the positive side, these regulations mean that in general the buses are on time, clean, well maintained and are comfortable, being fully air-conditioned.

Limenas bus station telephone number: 22162

Bus routes and cost guide

Thassos to Limenaria & Potos: 3.80€/4.00€

Limenaria to Thassos: 3.80€

Potos to Thassos via Prinos: 4.00€

Thassos to Theologos: 5.10€

Theologos to Thassos: 5.10€

Thassos to Skala Prinos: 1.80€

Skala Prinos to Thassos: 1.80€

Panagia to Thassos: 1.20€

Thassos to Panagia: 1.20€

Thassos to Skala Potamias: 1.50€

Skala Potamias to Thassos: 1.50€

Round the island via Prinos: 9.10€

Round the island via Panagia: 9.10€

Thassos to Aliki: 3.20€

Aliki to Thassos: 3.20€

Thassos to Kinira (Paradise Beach): 2.40€

Kinira (Paradise Beach) to Thassos: 2.20€

Limenaria to Theologos: 1.60€

Limenaria - Aliki & around the island: 9.10€

Potos to Theologos: 1.20€

Potos to Aliki & around the island: 9.10€

Aliki to Potos & Limenaria: 2.00€/2.30€

Thassos to Chrisi Amoudia (Golden Beach): 1.70€

Golden Beach to Thassos: 1.70€

Skala Prinos to Limenaria & Potos: 2.40€/2.60€

Prinos Village to Thassos: 1.90€

Prinos Village to Limenaria/Potos: 2.10€/2.40€

Skala Sotiras via Skala Prinos to Thassos: 2.10€

Skala Rachoni to Thassos: 1.20€

Skala Potamias to Aliki & around the island: 9.10€

Ferry and hydrofoil information

As with the buses, the ferry and hydrofoil timetables have a tendency to change without notice and are not usually published until May each year. This means that not only have I been unable in the past to guarantee accuracy, but it has also not been possible to publish in time for the spring and early summer visitors.

I have therefore decided to only outline in the following pages the general information that I hope will be of initial help. You can obtain the latest timetables from the ferry and Flying Dolphin terminals in Thassos Town, Skala Prinos and Kavala during your visit.

Ferries

There are two ferry companies on the island the red ferries (called the 'Fast Ferries') and the blue and red ferries (ANETH). The two ferry routes to the island are from Kavala to Skala Prinos and Keramoti to Thassos Town (Limenas), the latter servicing 'Alexander the Great Airport' (*Megas Alexandros)*.

Facilities on the ferries include a sun-deck (so have your suntan oil handy), internal air-conditioned lounge, cafeteria, toilets and on some of the ferries, stair-lifts have recently been installed for the elderly and infirmed.

On all ferries, smoking is permitted on the decks, but only two ferries (ANETH company) have a smoking area inside.

Kavala to Skala Prinos

From May to September services start at around 09:00hrs from Kavala and continue roughly every two to three hours until approx. 20:00hrs.

Keramoti to Thassos Town

From May to September, services start at 06:30hrs from Keramotti and continue roughly every one to two hours until 20:00hrs in May and September, 21:30hrs in June and 23:00hrs in July and August. There are reduced timetables for Sundays, early season and winter months.

If you are traveling by car, you should plan to be at the ferry port at least half hour before departure at normal times and at least an hour at weekends and holidays.

The crossing time is roughly 35 minutes from Keramotti to Thassos Town and 1 hr 35 minutes from Kavala to Skala Prinos. The bus timetables are linked to the ferries, so that when they dock, there should be a bus waiting to take you to either Thassos Town (if you have taken the Skala Prinos ferry), or from there onto your resort. This excludes the evening ferries, when you will have to continue your journey by taxi.

To give an idea of price, the charge for foot passengers (dependant on the ferry route), is between 2.50 and 3.50 euro, with cars costing between 11 and 20 euro dependant on the route and size of vehicle (car passengers are not included in the price).

Useful phone numbers for further information:-

Thassos Port Authority:	(0030) 2593 022355
Kavala Port Authority:	(0030) 2510 223716
Harbour Office Keramoti:	(0030) 2591 051098

Flying Dolphin hydrofoil

A hydrofoil service (foot-passengers only) is available from both Limenas and Skala Prinos to Kavala. Prices are 7 euro one-way, and 3.5 euro for children, with the journey taking around 35 minutes. The front section of the boats is non-smoking, but there is a smoking section at the rear. Although there is a bar, this is usually not open. The boat is entirely enclosed with aircraft style seating.

Below I have added examples of hydrofoil timetables, to be used mainly as a guide to frequency. As the situation with the hydrofoil times is the same as with the ferries and buses, in that they can change without prior notice, I advise that you check for the latest times before travelling.

Limenas - Kavala

From Limenas	From Kavala
08:55	08:00
15:30	14:00

Skala Prinos - Kavala

From Prinos	From Kavala
07:15	06:30
13:00	12:15

Eating and drinking

In this chapter I will first cover eating out and bars. During the writing of this book I have meticulously sought to be unbiased and accurate with all the information I have included. However, where eating out is concerned, we have all had the disappointing experience of a poor meal in a highly recommended restaurant! Both different tastes and changing circumstances can mean that a good restaurant to one person can be an awful one to others. Therefore in this chapter, I believe it is wise and fair not to recommend any particular restaurants or tavernas on the island, but instead try to outline some basic information and useful hints.

I will say that I have rarely had a poor meal on the island, but on that odd occasion, I have found it hard to complain when the average price of a meal is the equivalent of £10 - £12 per person.

The tips I would pass on are as follows:

First take a good look at the taverna or restaurant in question, is it busy, does it have pleasant surroundings? A major part of eating out on holiday is, I believe, the service, surroundings and views. Are the locals eating there, as they are more knowledgeable of the best eating-places and lastly, is the menu comprehensive? Don't be put off by the faded photographs of food outside the taverna, most are like this and if you were to stand outside in the sun all day you would fade too!

Service in most of the restaurants is good, if sometimes a little slow, especially when it comes to obtaining the bill, but remember you are on holiday, so relax. It is acceptable for you to ask to look at the food in the kitchen and enquire about any particular dish. You may feel a little wary at doing so, but whenever I have asked, they have been more than happy to show me around and answer any questions.

Most dishes come with French fries and/or rice and often with a small amount of salad. If you are partial to salad, it may be advisable to order an extra portion, but they are usually large, so one should be enough for two people.

If, after your main course you do not order a pudding, many tavernas will bring some melon, mousse, or jelly 'on the house' to thank you for your custom, or you will get a small glass of Ouzo or Metaxa with the bill. It is worth keeping an eye out to see what that particular taverna's approach is.

Beware of ordering non-Greek branded spirits or unusual liqueurs without asking the price first. On my first trip to Thassos, I ordered a Glayva and almost had to take out a mortgage to pay for it!

Most tavernas and restaurants are open all day serving breakfast, lunch and dinner. For those who want a more British start to the day, (I'm afraid I'm one of those), a well-cooked and comprehensive English breakfast can be obtained at many of the tavernas, with only the bacon being a little different (but very tasty). The cost with juice, tea/coffee, the usual egg, bacon, sausage, beans, tomatoes and toast is around 5 euro. The alternative of a continental breakfast is always available.

Lunch if you can manage it after breakfast, is usually a similar menu as evenings, but most places do snacks and salads as an alternative.

In the larger villages and especially Thassos Town and Limenaria, there are a number of 'fast food' outlets, where you can eat in, or buy a take away such as a rotisserie chicken, kebab, or burger meal. If you are feeling a little 'homesick', there is even a fish and chips shop run by expats in the back streets of Thassos Town.

One word of warning though, in hotels and apartments that have a restaurant or bar-food facilities, the management tend to frown upon guests eating their own food in the rooms. I would also advise that where it is acceptable, it is courteous to dispose of any food waste yourself and not leave it for the hotel cleaning staff.

There are two small clubs in Thassos town, namely 'Just in Time' and 'Davidoff', both are on the same street just off the main pedestrian area. They 'liven up' around 10:00 pm and go on until around 6:00 am.

A quick guide to Greek food

To help with the menu, I have outlined below a list of dishes you will usually find.

Appetisers

Mezes - A plate containing a selection of different appetisers, similar to the Spanish tapas, usually to be shared around the table. Mezes can include seafood, meats, vegetable dishes and dips.

Dolmades (or stuffed vine leaves) - vine leaves stuffed with rice and then rolled (a hot variation also contains minced meat). Served most often cold as an appetiser, but can also be served hot with an avgolemono sauce on top. Its origin is thought to be from Thebes about the time of Alexander the Great.

Prawn Cocktail - Similar to the old style UK version with salad and cocktail sauce, but usually a very large portion.

Taramosalata - Greek caviar combined with breadcrumbs, oil, onion, and lemon juice to compliment any meal as an appetiser. This is a thick pink or white puree of fish roe, dependent on the type of fish. Sometimes mashed potato is substituted for breadcrumbs.

Tzatziki - A yoghurt, cucumber and garlic dip to be served chilled on its own, or with pita or plain bread. Great on a gyro.

Keftedes - Small rissoles or fritters, often made with minced lamb, pork or veal, onion, egg and herbs and sometimes with ouzo as a moistener. Keftedes are shaped into flattened balls and usually fried.

Main courses

Roast Lamb - Lamb prepared in the traditional Greek way with garlic inserted into the meat and cooked with bay leaves.

Roast Chicken - Both from an oven or a spit, cooked in olive oil. I personally think the rotisserie chickens are the best and taste as chicken should taste. Chicken in most restaurants on the island tends to be in fillet form, however, one of the few villages where chicken on the bone is served outside Thassos Town is Panagia, although you see many empty rotisseries and no, I don't know why.

Moussaka - A Greek national dish, Moussaka is prepared with sliced eggplant, lean ground beef, onions, tomatoes, butter, eggs, milk, cheese and seasonings and baked in an oven.

Gyro - Thin slices of barbecued meat specially seasoned with herbs and spices, served with tomatoes and onions on pita bread, and topped with tzatziki. Best from a rotisserie.

Pastitsio - A Greek 'Lasagne' combining macaroni, minced meat, cheese and covered with béchamel sauce.

Pilafi - Fluffy rice simmered in butter, spices and rich chicken stock.

Souvlaki - Souvlaki are made from cubes of meat that have been marinated for several hours in olive oil, lemon juice & rigani (Greek oregano), then threaded on wooden skewers and grilled or barbequed. They are usually made from beef, chicken, lamb, pork, or veal.

Stifado - Stifado is a casserole made of beef, veal or lamb in wine with pearl onions, tomatoes, herbs and spices.

Kleftico - or 'Klephtiko' is a term that refers to any kind of meat dish that is sealed and baked. The word comes from the time of the Greek revolution, when bands of Greek guerrillas, called Klephts, hid in the mountains and cooked their dinner in pits sealed with mud, so that smoke and steam would not escape and betray their position. Usually it will be Lamb Kleftico that is on the menu.

Spanakopitta - Spanakopitta is a spinach pie, about the size of a flan. These small pies are made with a spinach and feta cheese filling in filo pastry. They can also be called spanakotiropitakia. However, they are referred to as Spanakopittes in Greek bakeries and I shall do likewise.

Stamnato - Usually made with lamb (or spelt 'lamp' or 'lab' ....one reason why I love the Greeks!) with potatoes in tomato and garlic sauce, baked in a traditional pot called a Lamm.

Pasta

Spaghetti Bolognese is a firm favourite on most menus (and they usually do it very well), but other pasta dishes are normally available.

Grilled meats

Grilled meat usually includes lamb chops, pork, veal and chicken, either plain or in a variety of sauces dependant on the restaurant.

Omelettes

Most tavernas offer a variety of omelettes on their menu.

Pizzas

Where pizzas are concerned there are some tavernas that specialise, having the proper ovens and expertise. So my advice would be to ask around to find the best place to go, but personally I have found most are at least equivalent in quality to the best in the UK.

Seafood

As with the majority of Mediterranean countries, in Greece you can find a wide variety of fresh and tasty seafood, before ordering though, I suggest you ask if the fish is fresh and not frozen. Many restaurants and tavernas have a chilled fresh seafood cabinet near the entrance and the waiters are usually happy to confirm the range of fresh fish they have on offer.

If you fancy splashing out on a lobster dinner, those restaurants that have fresh lobster on their menu usually require 24 hrs notice; I would also ask what the price would be per person and not per kilo. If you order prawns, the average price is around 10 euro and you get about six, king-sized and in their shells.

Patisseries

Melomakarona - A honey cookie sprinkled with a spice-nut mixture.

Koulouria - Also called Koulourakia - Tasty bread rings coated in sesame seeds.

Baklava - Nut filled, paper-thin layers of glazed filo pastry soaked in pure honey, make this the king of pastry desserts. Every country in the near-east claims baklava is its own.

Kourabiedes - Sugar covered crescent shaped cakes that melt in your mouth. They are usually served at weddings, at Christmas, and on special occasions, such as birthdays and holidays.

Diples - Honey rolls so thin and flaky that they crumble when they are bitten.

Kataifi - A delicious pastry made of shredded filo pastry rolled with nuts and honey and sprinkled with syrup. Found throughout the Mediterranean.

Loukoumades - Feathery light honey tokens or sweet fritters, deep fried to a golden brown and dipped in boiling honey. A tasty delight from ancient Greece where they were given as tokens to winners of the games at festivals.

Halva - Is a candy made from ground sesame seeds. It is an oriental originated sweet, popular in Greece.

Coffee

Greek style coffee - This is a thick, powdered coffee that is made in a brickee (or brika), which is traditionally a small brass pot with a long handle. Modern advances have given us stainless steel brikas. This is not instant coffee, and even though powdered, the coffee used does not dissolve. The grounds settle to the bottom of the cup. When you order Greek coffee, you must specify plain, sweet or medium-sweet (sketo, glyko or metrio in Greek, respectively).

You can also order Cappuccino, Expresso and other types of coffee in most restaurants. Tea is usually available, but it comes in a do-it yourself style and can taste a little odd due to the long-life milk often used. I would recommend you ask for fresh milk.

Bars

There are a wide range of bars in all the towns and resorts, from the traditional 'men only' Greek bars, through disco-bars, cocktail bars and those run by ex-pats that offer a snack menu, usually including English breakfast served in the morning.

The vast majority of the bars have satellite TV and offer live coverage of sporting events such as major football matches.

All stock a wide range of drinks at reasonable prices. Most of the international lagers are available, such as Stella, Heineken and Amstel, but I would certainly recommend Mythos, one of the local Greek brews.

Supermarkets

The supermarkets in the resorts and main towns are well provisioned for the foreign holidaymaker. Many brands are recognisable and if not, the supermarket staff are usually very helpful. Milk comes in cartons and although in Greek, just look out for the picture of a cow and the colour coding is the same as in the UK. Crisps are known as chips in Greece (and just for your information, chips are known as French Fries).

If you want to eat in, supermarkets usually have a wide range of vegetables and fruit on sale, but meat, other than the basics such as cooked cold meats and bacon have to be bought from the local butcher, just ask and they will tell you where it is.

There are take-aways in the main resorts with a range of food, but if you don't have the facilities to cook meat in your accommodation, many tavernas and restaurants (if you ask nicely) will do a take-away service for main meat items such as a roast chicken.

If you want bread or pastries for later on in the day, I would advise you buy them early, as the supermarkets tend to sell out before lunchtime.

All the supermarkets sell wines and spirits (the Thassian wines are very good), with again most of the brands we are used to back home, available on the island. The selection of lagers is international, however the Greek lagers, such as Mythos are in *my view* excellent. In addition to the supermarkets, there are usually dedicated off-licences in the main resorts that stock an even greater range. Prices are at least comparable with the UK, if not cheaper.

Shopping

Mens' clothes and shoes

As with most products on Thassos, clothes and shoes are cheaper than in the UK. However, the selection of modern men's wear is poor and you really need to go to the mainland for a good choice. There is a greater range of men's shoes although still limited (especially where fashion designs are concerned), but the prices are reasonable and you may be able to pick up a real bargain.

Cigarettes, sweets and newspapers

In all the towns and resorts you will notice large wooden kiosks on the pavements of the main streets. This is where in Greece you traditionally buy such items as cigarettes and tobacco, newspapers, magazines, ice-cream, drinks, sweets and snacks such as crisps. The supermarkets also sell all of these except usually newspapers.

If you smoke, don't bother bringing any with you (and remember Greece is in the EU, so you won't be able to purchase them in the duty free at your UK airport) as they are vastly cheaper than back home, at approx. 3.00 euro for a packet of 20 (£2.30). You needn't shop around as the price will be the same at all the outlets. All the main brands are available such as Marlboro, Rothmans, Superkings, Benson & Hedges, etc. As you will be aware, UK airports as with all public buildings, are now totally smoke-free zones and on landing in Greece the rule applies until you get into the luggage collection area.

For those who become homesick whilst away and want to know what new stealth taxes the government have imposed, English newspapers are available, although they will sometimes be the previous day's edition. I have personally seen on sale The Daily Mail, The Mirror, The Sun and a couple of the main broadsheets, so you should have a good choice.

English magazines are more rare, but I have seen some of the main women's publications on the newsstands.

Souvenirs

Well this is a difficult subject to write about as we all have a different view of what a good souvenir is. In all the resorts on the island there are a myriad of shops selling the more 'colourful' items and as you will see many explicit statues of well endowed male gods! If you look around though, there are some quality goods available as presents and souvenirs at reasonable prices. Gold jewellery is good value as are leather goods and if you really get stuck, there is always the bottle of Ouzo, Metaxa or some honey.

Personal electronic items

Whilst the choice of electronic items is as good as anywhere, especially in Kavala, the price comparison with the same item back in the UK is more variable. The weakening of Sterling has not helped, but even prior to this, some items were less expensive, whilst others were comparable. As Greece is in the European Union, one advantage is if you find a bargain, you won't pay duty on it when you return home.

My advice is if you are contemplating buying anything electronic, it may be worth putting off that purchase and checking whilst you are over here. Remember though, it may be a problem if the goods turn out to be faulty. So if you do intend to purchase expensive items, check first that the manufacturer's guarantee will cover the item back home.

With regard to cosmetics, fashion, hairdressers and jewellery, I will pass this section over to my partner Carol.

Cosmetics

Although Thassos is a small island, as far as buying your moisturiser, body lotion, shampoo etc. and the all-important sunscreen you don't have to worry. Especially in the towns there is a good selection of retailers that stock a wide range of cosmetics and toiletries.

Pharmacies and supermarkets especially have an extensive range of known brands ... Nivea Visage, Garnier, Dove, L'Oreal to name but a few, as well as basics such as Johnsons. If you cannot find the UK product you want there are Greek equivalent brands available with no compromise on quality and often at cheaper prices. So no need to waste valuable space and weight in your suitcase, just buy all you need when you arrive.

Hairdressers

There are salons in Thassos Town, some of the larger villages and Kavala to cater for all your follicle needs, and after a few days in the sun and sea. What better way to treat your hair, and yourself, than having a few hours relaxation and pampering, preparing for your evening out in one of the many restaurants and tavernas.

Fashion

Thassos Town has an array of different shops to cater for every taste and age group selling all you will need for your stay on Thassos. On my first visit I made the mistake of buying my holiday clothes in the UK only to find, there was so much more choice in Thassos Town and a lot cheaper. Leather shoes and handbags are also extremely good value.... visit 'Leather Lane' in Thassos Town, an Aladdin's Cave of handbags, holdalls and suitcases, in a wide range of colours and sizes.

Jewellery

It seems that nearly every shop you pass in Thassos Town and the larger villages sell some kind of jewellery - bangles, bracelets, rings, necklaces, earrings and much more. There is an amazing choice for every age and at modest prices. You could buy a different piece for each night of your holiday. I especially like the designs created from brightly coloured coral and shell.

For that special gift or holiday souvenir, you can visit the specialised jewellery shops in the heart of Thassos Town. Here you will find a wide range of gold and silver jewellery, with some retailers designing and manufacturing their own unique ranges. You may see something to treasure and keep as a memory of our beautiful island and you never know, perhaps add to on your next visit to Thassos.

H.M. Customs

Regarding taking goods back home, if the goods you are carrying has had tax paid in Greece, you do not have to pay any tax or duty on them in the UK. Any alcohol or tobacco you bring in must be for your own use and transported by you.

Own use' includes goods for your own consumption and gifts. If you bring in goods for resale, or for any payment, even payment in kind, they are regarded as being for a commercial purpose.

With regards to quantities allowed, you are particularly likely to be asked questions by customs officers if you have more than:

3200 cigarettes, 200 cigars, 400 cigarillos, 3 kg tobacco, 110 litres of beer, 90 litres of wine, 10 litres of spirits, 20 litres of fortified wine (such as port or sherry).

Some goods are banned, such as plant materials that could contain diseases.

Sports and recreation

Fishing

Fishing is a popular pastime on the island for the locals, both by boat and off-shore, but for those visitors who would like to relax and try their luck with a rod and tackle, then most of the main resorts have a shop selling fishing tackle and bait.

It is often the local hardware retailer or similar, that doubles up as a fishing shop and although I am not an experienced fisherman, I have been surprised at the quality and range of gear on offer and the low cost of the items. To give an idea to the interested reader, a good extendable rod is only around 15 euro.

The sea around the island abounds with a wide variety of fish, a fact that confirms the absence of pollution. The species include mullet, bream, blackfish, grey pandora, picarel and horse mackerel, with molluscs and crustaceans such as octopus and lobster.

Boat hire

Small outboard boats can be hired from some of the beaches on an hr/day basis. These include Skala Sotiras, Potos, Pefkari and Golden Beach. An example of cost is approx. 60 - 80 euro per day for a boat from 'Albatros' in Pefkari, or 'Aldebaran' in Potos.

Larger sea going boats can be hired on the island on a daily or weekly basis. To give you an example, a Sea Ray 29 foot cruiser with two inboard diesel engines, which is based in Thassos Town (Hotel Pegasus), sleeps 4, or for a day cruise will accommodate 6. The price per day (10:00 – 18:00) including a skipper and fuel is 150 euro plus food, or 250 euro per day for an overnight rental.

The sea going Eros II offers daily boat excursions (excluding Monday). For example, every Wednesday and Sunday it sails around the island. There is a barbeque on board and the trip lasts from 10:00 until 17:45, the cost is 30 euro p.p., children half price. The Eros II desk can be found in the old harbour of Thassos Town.

Paragliding

There is paragliding on Pefkari, Golden Beach and Skala Potamias. The company supplies safety equipment.

Jet skis

Jet skis are available for hire on a number of beaches, these include Golden Beach, Potos, Pefkari and Paradise Beach.

Banana boats and donuts

For those not conversant with this activity, a banana boat is a long thin inflatable with seats for the participants positioned down its length. The 'banana' is towed behind a speedboat and the objective is to stay on and enjoy the ride. Donuts are an alternative to the banana and are large inflatable rings towed behind the boat.

Banana boat and donut rides can be found at a number of beaches including Pefkari, Golden Beach and Skala Potamias. For safety's sake it is important that you wear the life jacket supplied.

Windsurfing

Windsurfing is available at many of the larger beaches including, Skala Rachoni, Golden Beach, Paradise Beach and Pefkari.

Sub-aqua

To my knowledge there is only one certified dive-centre on Thassos, namely Vasiliadis Diving Club in Potos. Their office is on the main pedestrian precinct that runs behind and parallel with the seafront. I have been told the instructors at Vasiliadis are very professional and go out of their way to help all levels of diving experience.

I have also heard of another company elsewhere, but be warned, apparently it is not certified and therefore illegal.

Horse riding

Horse riding is available on the island at the following stables:-

Pine Tree Paddock near Skala Rachoni, look for the yellow signs on the main road.

Pegasus Riding Stables in Theologos offer outdoor-riding, riding-tours in small groups, pony and donkey riding for the children and therapy riding.

Walking

For those who enjoy walking or rambling, Thassos offers some beautiful walks with magnificent scenery. My advice would be to obtain a copy of 'Walking on Thassos' by Truus Van de Mast and Roos Gruwel, or 'Walks in Northeast Thassos' by Lance Chilton. Copies of both books can be obtainable from Val's Leather World in Limenas. The books contain comprehensive information on the island and 'guides' you through a wide variety of quality walks around the island. Troos and Roos moved to Thassos in 1987 and Roos is a nature guide for the Dutch Nature organisation on Thassos, sadly Truus died in 1998. Finally at least one of the major tour operators offer a one day guided walk (adults only) which costs around 30 euro per person.

Cycling

There are a number of cycle hire shops on the island, so I suggest you ask at your hotel/apartments, they should be able to give you directions to the nearest. In Potos there is the Yannis Reizis Hotel, that specialise in mountain biking holidays. They can supply the bikes (rental by the day or week) and all the equipment as well as guides for the best routes on the island. They cater for downhillers, XC freeriding and tour cycling. The hotel organises the yearly 'Thassos Cup Race' around the island, which attracts riders from all over Europe in April.

Spa and fitness

The Alexandra Beach Resort (see 'The beaches and resorts' page 97) is open to non-residents and has a full selection of spa facilities such as a Jacuzzi, massage, facial and body treatments, manicures and a Gym.

If a day at a spa is attractive to you, I would suggest that you phone the resort prior to a visit, to confirm the cost and availability.

Tel. no. : (25930) 58000

Money matters

There are four main banks in Thassos town and two in Limenaria. In Thassos Town branches of the ATE, ETE, Emporiki and Eurobank are to be found in the town centre. In Limenaria there are branches of ETE and ATE banks. All the main banks have an ATM (hole in the wall), which take most debit and credit cards.

The charges for the use of your card will for the most part depend on your bank back home, so it might be wise to have a discussion with your bank/building society before you leave and confirm the costs you will incur for withdrawals. If you use one of the banks on the island to exchange Sterling or travellers cheques (and this may also be the case with the alternatives below), take your passport with you to confirm your identity.

Other than the banks, there are a wide range of exchange options, many hotels, shops and car hire companies will also exchange Sterling, but make sure you check the rate and any charges first. Again the Greeks are very honest and I have never been short-changed, but the rates can vary, so 'better safe than sorry'.

In the banks, you may find a queue (remember life is at a slow pace in Greece), look round, as there may be a ticket-machine where you can retrieve a number identifying your place in the queue.

As to the exchange rate, I certainly have found that it is generally equal or better than that found back in the UK, so if you don't want the hassle of picking up currency before you leave home, just bring Sterling and change it on the island (e.g. in September 2007 the exchange rate in the UK was 1.38, on the island it was 1.42).

Credit/Debit cards are not accepted in most tavernas and smaller shops on the island, so it is advisable to carry sufficient money with you on days and evenings out. One further point regarding drawing cash out abroad via a credit card (learnt from personal experience), is that many card companies will not only charge you a relatively high exchange commission, but also an additional cash advance fee. So if you want to use your credit card abroad, I would therefore advise you check on potential charges before leaving home.

With regard to the safety of carrying money and leaving it in your room, as I have stressed before, the Greeks are extremely honest and over the last 30 years of travelling in Greece, I have never had anything stolen. On the contrary, I have accidentally left valuable items in public places, only to find them untouched hours later.... but remember, there are not only Greeks on the island!

At the time of going to press, a helpful hint to remember is that 10 euro equals approximately £8.

The bank opening hours are Monday to Friday, 08:00-14:00/14:30. However, if you are exchanging money, it is advisable to be at the bank well before closing time.

Phone numbers: (Thassos prefix : 25930)

National Bank of Greece (ETE)
Limenas : 22436
Limenaria : 52978

Emporiki Bank
Limenas : 22883
Potos : 22703
Skala Potamias : 22703

Agricultural Bank of Greece (ATE)
Limenas : 22940, 22970
Limenaria : 51382, 52683

Weather

What can you say about the weather in Greece other than as a 'Brit' I find it invariably gorgeous. To be a little more accurate, what we would call summer back in the UK usually starts in May with temperatures rising throughout the following months (see the table below). Through late April, May and early June, and then again in October, the weather can be compared to a good British summer.

The months of July and August tend to be the hottest, with daily temperatures often reaching the 90's. The high temperatures can spark off thunderstorms in the evening, but these are not usually accompanied by rain and are more entertaining than a nuisance.

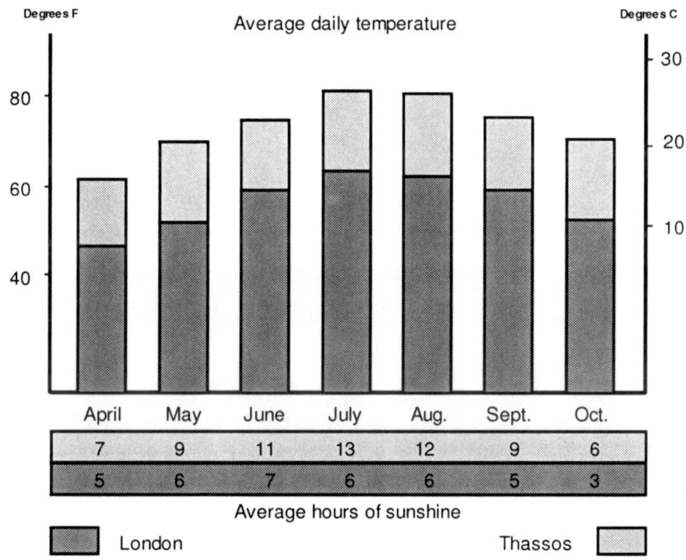

The Meltemi

The Meltemi (the Greek equivalent of the French Mistral) is a powerful wind that blows across all of the Aegean islands. It is the result of a high-pressure system over the Balkans and a low-pressure system over Turkey, creating strong northeast winds. The Meltemi occurs mainly during the summer with July and August being the worst affected months, but it can spring up occasionally in May and October. It usually starts in the early afternoon and can die out at sunset although occasionally, it will last through the night and repeat for three to six, sometimes even ten days. Northern islands including Thassos are less affected than those in the south of the Aegean, which can suffer from summer gales, particularly disruptive on north facing beaches. Ferry sailings and boat trips can be cancelled, sunbathing can be unpleasant and your nights sleep disturbed, however on Thassos, I have never found it a problem. Remember though not to leave valuables on the balcony, or you may return to find them 'Gone with the Wind!

In September the evenings begin to cool, but that can be a blessing for those who enjoy a good night's sleep. Temperatures continue to drop into October and through to December and in January and February there can be the 'real Thassos winter' with snowfalls that can result (as in 2006) in drifting of up to 2 metres. The snow stays 'white' and usually only lasts a couple of days, causing little disruption.

This time of the year is welcomed by ski lovers such as Carol and myself, as it offers the opportunity of crossing over to the mainland to visit one of the nearby winter sports resorts and experience the fun and exercise that can be realised at the other end of the temperature scale.

Thassos receives a generous rainfall during the winter months, but rather than a problem this is a blessing for Thassos, resulting in the luxuriant vegetation of the island (compared with other Greek islands) and the abundant and clean water supply, as you will see if you visit the village of Panagia.

The long-range weather forecast for 2008, is that the summer is expected to be very hot and dry. I would therefore suggest that those who are sensitive to high temperatures book accommodation that includes air-conditioning.

This chapter allows me the opportunity to explain that although the photograph on the back cover of this book makes me look like I have a terminal case of sunburn, it is just down to the printing process and in normal life I look less like a lobster!

Bugs, biters and things

This chapter is not for the paranoid, as I have been 'true to my word' adding a definitive list of the bugs and biters on the island. That does not mean that any of the following are a threat to 'life and limb' and I can confirm that regarding all listed, I have never met anyone who has suffered more than the usual 'mozzy' bites or the very rare wasp sting, so with that in mind, here we go.

Mosquitoes

There is the usual problem of mosquitoes on the island, but a good covering of mosquito repellent in the evenings, which is sold at all supermarkets, should generally protect you. It does seem to be dependent on the person, I rarely get bitten, whereas my partner Carol seems to attract all the little critters. Her answer is she has better quality blood!

I would advise you to use a mosquito machine in your bedroom, which can be the old plug-in heated tablet type (the tablets are still available), or the new heated liquid system. After testing the latter, they are in my view superior, one bottle of liquid should last for the whole holiday and there are no fiddly tablets to change every day.

Mosquito bites

Although there are 'over the counter' remedies available at the local pharmacies, you could try applying vinegar to the bites and you will find the itchiness will subside.

Wasps

A more irritating insect can be the wasp. The island does suffer from larger numbers in certain areas than in the UK and if (as in 2006) there is a low rainfall in the preceding winter, it can cause a mini-plague. They tend to be found in greater numbers near the populated beaches (where there is a good supply of tourist food), with the areas around towns and villages having very few if any. So it is dependant on where you are and what you are doing. However, don't worry.... the locals don't.... try to ignore them, I certainly haven't been stung and just find them irritating at times.....another answer is to buy a fly swat and see how many you can exterminate. Sorry, I apologise to the entomologists amongst you.

On some beaches, eating at the beachside tavernas can be a trial, but ask the waiter for a 'burner' (smouldering Greek coffee in a container....yes it seems it has to be Greek), which is a great deterrent to the little blighters. The good news is (if there is a plague), that come sundown they all return to their nest.

At the time of going to press, the prognosis looks good for 2008. Due to the very cold winter spell and good rainfall, there should not be a plague this year.

Hornets

There are hornets on Thassos, but small numbers mean they are not a problem. They have a fearsome reputation for stinging and causing considerable harm, but in fact individually, they are just as harmful as a wasp or bee - no more and no less. Like most bees and wasps they usually only sting if you are blocking a flight path or are moving rapidly. However, nests should be avoided at all costs as a swarm attack can be serious! For those not familiar with hornets, they have similar colouring to a wasp (being a member of the wasp family), but are about twice the size. The only nest I have seen on the island was at the far end of the promontory at Aliki.

Ants

There are ants of course on the island and they remind me of the 'Fire Ants' of the southern states of America. Leave any food out in easy reach and you may return to find a long procession of thousands of the critters offloading it back to their nest. It can be quite an entertainment, watching them manhandle something many times their size and never giving up.

Scorpions

Scorpions.... I've never seen one on Thassos although I have occasionally seen them on other islands, but don't worry, in the most unlikely event that you would be stung, it is said to be no worse than that of a bee.

Snakes

With regard to snakes, I have only seen one that was crossing the road and I saw it too late. It is now a flat-snake! There are a number of species on the island as in all of Greece, but only one is poisonous, namely the Viper. Most vipers are nocturnal and are only sporadically observed in the daylight, when they bask or mate. It is easy to distinguish a viper from the harmless species, based on their triangular head, 'swollen' cheeks, stout body (vipers are seldom longer than 1metre) and the characteristic zig-zag pattern on their back. A viper bite is not necessarily poisonous: in only about 30% of bites there is actual injection of venom, and thus a need for treatment.

The rule is if you see a snake, be on the safe-side and leave it well alone, but *please* be assured, it is extremely rare to hear of a bite. The precautions that can be taken are that when out walking in long grass, wear ankle length boots and do not turn large stones over, or place your hand into crevices that might be home to a snake. If you were to be the 'one in a million' and are bitten, the advice is to be safe and seek medical help straight away.

Sea Urchins

Sea urchins can be found in some areas on the island (as with most of the Mediterranean), but if you have children, a quick chat at one of the beach tavernas, or a scan for their remains on the beach will confirm whether to take precautions. If they are around the simplest solution is to wear flip-flops when entering the sea.

If you do step on one, consult a doctor or pharmacist and they will advise you on the best course of action. However don't worry, it will usually mean nothing more serious than a little discomfort.

Here is the advice given in a medical journal:-

- Look for the signs and symptoms of a sea urchin sting: small spines embedded in the skin; a localized brownish-purple colour where the barbs made contact with the skin.
- Use sterile tweezers to remove any embedded spines.
- Control bleeding by applying direct pressure to the wound.
- Irrigate the wound with an irrigation syringe.
- Clean the wound with a disinfectant solution.
- Immerse the foot in hot water for at least 30 minutes, until pain subsides.
- Elevate the foot to control swelling.
- Dress the wound with a sterile bandage.
- Monitor for signs of infection. These signs include swelling, redness, pus, red lines radiating from the site of the wound, heat at the site of the wound, and fever.
- Seek medical advice.

Jellyfish stings

If you do experience a sting, the quickest remedy is applying urine to the affected area, so pick your holiday companions carefully!

Health

Hospitals, doctors & community clinics

Whereas we all hope that nothing untoward happens on our holidays, especially health wise, as I can personally testify it sometimes does.

My view of the island's facilities is a good one, with all but the most serious incidents catered for on the island itself. In Prinos there is a health centre, which in fact is a small hospital, well equipped and easy to find by following the signs in the village. On the mainland in Kavala, there is a modern and fully equipped hospital for more serious health issues.

There are also private doctors in Thassos Town and Limenaria. Here it is also possible to find a dentist, an orthopaedic surgeon, a cardiologist and general practitioner. In the smaller villages they have a weekly surgery (check for details). Normally the surgery is near the middle of the village and can be recognised by a red cross on the door or on a sign in front of the building.

The pharmacies on Thassos operate at regular business hours (usually 08:00 - 15:00 and 18:00 - 24:00) and you will find one in the towns and villages listed below. One pharmacy stays open during the night and the early morning hours (check locally for details). The quality of medicines and advice is equal to that back in the UK. In one pharmacy in the square in Thassos Town, the pharmacist Dimitri, speaks fluent English and is very helpful and caring and if necessary will advise you on where you can get further advice or help.

There are pharmacies in the following towns and villages:
Thassos Town
Skala Kallirachis
Prinos
Limenaria
Potos
Panagia

For emergencies there is a twenty-four hour doctor service at the health center in Prinos. Alternatively there are private doctors you can visit if the need arises.

Remember, if you are a UK citizen, you should apply for an NHS distributed European Health Insurance Card (EHIC) as the previous E111 form is no longer valid. This will allow you to obtain free or reduced cost treatment abroad; this includes only treatment provided on the state scheme. The EHIC is free of charge and can be obtained in the following ways. I advise that you apply well in advance of your trip, as it can take a week or two for the card to arrive:

By internet at **www.ehic.org.uk**
By telephone on 0845 6062030
Or by form from the Post Office

Dental services

My own personal experience of ill health on Thassos was in 2005, prior to moving to the island to live. Only hours after arriving on the island, I was stricken by severe toothache and although I suffered for two further days (I'm a man), in the end I had to ask for help and was recommended to a dentist in Thassos Town.

All I can say is that I was amazed at the care shown to me on my arrival and the quality of the subsequent treatment. The surgery was modern, comfortable and very well equipped and the dentist friendly, he spoke fluent English and his 'chair-side' manner was highly professional. I also found on my return to the UK, that the charges I had paid, were less than half that I would have paid at home. All in all, I have to say that if I required dental work, I would prefer to have it done on Thassos, rather than back in the UK.

Phone numbers:

General Hospital of Kavala	: (2510) 292000
Health Centre in Prinos	: 71100, 71498 (incl. Emergency)

Community clinics:

Thassos Town (Limenas)	: 22222
Theologos	: 31211
Limenaria	: 51235
Panagia	: 61203

Doctors phone numbers:

Limenas	: 22100
Panagia	: 62238
Potomia	: 61155 (Tuesdays & Fridays)
Potos	: 53233
Skala Sotiras	: 71332 (Thursdays)
Kallirachis	: 91221
Limenaria	: 53333
Theologos	: 31211

Traditional remedies

Sunburn

The most obvious advice anyone can give is 'don't get burned in the first place'! If like most, you are not used to the Mediterranean sun, take it very easy on the first few days and use plenty of high factor sun-block cream. You are especially vulnerable when there is a breeze, or when you are travelling in an open top car (a point I learnt from bitter experience), as you do not feel the full extent of your skin's reaction to the sun.

If the worst does happen, my first advice is go to the local pharmacy and seek help. If this is not possible, a cold shower will initially relieve the pain, but drip dry, as using a towel will only aggravate the situation. For mild sunburn, cool compresses with equal parts of milk and water may suffice. Another remedy, recommended by many, is to spray or pat the effected areas with white or cider vinegar; this will relieve the pain and itching and hopefully give you a good night's sleep until you can visit a pharmacy.

The symptoms may also be relieved by taking asprin or ibuprofen, but do not exceed the doses specified on the label.

Stomach upset

If the worst happens, try adding a little fresh lemon juice to a Greek coffee and knock it back (so you don't taste it) and in no time at all the symptoms will ease.

Safety

Where safety is concerned, the subject falls into two categories.

First there is the safety aspect with regard to crime; one of the points that has always attracted me to Greece, especially the islands, is the lack of both property and personal crime. It does exist, or there wouldn't be police or prisons in Greece, but as far as the tourist is concerned it is almost non-existent. What property crime does exist, tends to be committed by less desirable tourists and opportunist criminals from nearby poorer states. If you see the police on the island they will usually be drinking coffee or chatting to colleagues. But be warned, if you do transgress the rules, the police can be quite heavy handed.

The advice is of course be careful, however, I have accidentally left expensive items in public places in the past, only to return many hours later to find them just where I left them.

With regard to valuable items and money left in your accommodation, again I have never heard of any problems. The room cleaning staff, I have met in the past, have proved totally honest and as long as you lock the windows and doors you should have no need to worry.

In the event of a loss of a valuable item, remember that if you are insured, your insurance company will need written confirmation that the loss was reported to the local police.

One big advantage of Thassos especially for families and the more 'mature' traveller is that the island is not an attractive destination for the young 'Ibiza' style tourist. I can honestly say, I have never seen anyone on the island causing trouble or 'worse for wear'.

The second category is safety with respect to the activities you participate in during your stay. Safety in Greece is less stringently 'policed' than in the UK, so when you are out and about, and especially with children, extra care should be taken. To give an example, the railings around the battlements of Kavala Castle are well below the quality we would expect to find in the UK.

Being abroad you should also take extra care when driving. Although the Thassians are mostly good drivers, compared to say the Italians, if you are not experienced at driving on the right, mistakes can easily be made. It is a sobering sight on your travels, to see so many memorial boxes by the side of the road, especially on the cliff roads around the island!

As far as scooters and motorbikes are concerned, these are the most dangerous modes of transport on the island. You will see these being driven correctly with the riders wearing crash helmets, but usually only with shorts and T-shirts being worn......and I have seen the damage tarmac and gravel can do to human flesh!

One further point is not to trust the zebra crossings, in Greece these mean little although the rules do give the pedestrian the 'right of way'.

Hints and tips

Currency conversion

An easy way to convert euro to pounds is to remember that 10 euro is roughly £8.

Spelling

On your travels and in printed material (such as signs and menus), you will see names and places spelt in a variety of different ways. Do not be put off by the spelling, especially when you are trying to find somewhere, if it sounds the same, it probably is, e.g. roast lamp = roast lamb. I have to say though that I have great admiration for the islanders, not only have they had to deal with learning a foreign language, but one with a different alphabet too.

Sunbeds and parasols

If you are going to be a regular visit to the beach, rather than hire a parasol at an average of about 2.50 euro a day, it may be cost-effective to buy one from one of the beachside supermarkets (between 10 and 15 euro). If you don't have a car and you are put off at the thought of carrying it back to your accommodation each day, you can ask nicely at the supermarket where you purchased it and they may allow you to leave it there overnight.

The same goes with the sunbeds; a good lilo can be purchased for around 10 euro (a sunbed is between 2 and 3 euro a day) and gives you the added advantage of being able to use it in the sea. Many supermarkets have a compressor that they may allow you to use, so you can deflate it at the end of the day and take it back to your accommodation, or as before, ask nicely at the supermarket and they may allow you to leave it there.

Internet café

Most towns and resorts on the island have an Internet café, ask where your local one is. The cost is around 2 euro an hour, which makes it a cost effective alternative to 'phoning home' and a way of retrieving your emails while you are away. But remember to bring your important email addresses with you.

Mobile phones

Many mobile phone companies now offer reduced cost call packages for when you are abroad, but you will have to contact them and enquire what offers are available at the time of your trip. Also remember to get your phone unblocked for international calls before you leave home and when you are phoning or texting, you need to add the international pre-fix to the number you are calling.

Telephoning

Many apartments and hotels now have phones in the rooms, however, the cost of phoning home can be high. It may therefore be cost effective to text relatives with your room telephone number and ask them to phone you. Remember Greece is two hours ahead of UK time.

There are also a number of companies offering a reduced (and in some cases vastly reduced) cost of international calls, by entering a pre-fix number when calling home, or when calling from the UK to Greece. I would advise you to go on the web and check these out before leaving for Thassos. One such company is called 'firstnumber.co.uk', but there are many to choose from.

Public telephones are to be found throughout the island, but remember, even in this age of mobile phones, there can be a queue of holidaymakers waiting to phone home, especially in resorts in the early evening.

To phone the UK the prefix is 0044 and you drop the first zero of the UK number, i.e. a London number that starts 020.....would translate into 0044 20....

To phone Greece from the UK and elsewhere, the prefix is 0030.

One further option for phoning home is to use Skype, although a number of the Internet Cafes have Skype loaded (one that certainly has is in Thassos Town on the corner of Octovriou and K. Dimitriadi), it is best to bring a headset or Skype phone with you, as not all cafes supply them. If you are familiar with Skype, you will know that phone calls home will only cost cents, compared with euros with alternative services.

Batteries

All the modern battery sizes are available in the supermarkets at equivalent or cheaper prices than back home, but make sure you bring the battery chargers for your mobile phone, pda, etc.

Electricity

The electricity on Thassos and throughout Greece is 220V and therefore compatible with UK equipment. You can purchase the two pin adaptors at many local shops. So if you do not already own one, it may be cheaper to purchase them on the island.

Water

The tap water on Thassos is totally drinkable, as the island is self sufficient in fresh water (as you will see if you visit Panagia). If you have a preference for bottled water you can find it at all supermarkets, restaurants, cafeterias and kiosks. Why incur the expense, it may even be bottled from local spring water?

Bottled Water

In restaurants you may find a bottle of water on the table. The cost will be automatically added to your bill, so beware if you haven't opened it, ask for the charge to be credited. This usually only applies to restaurants on the mainland such as in Kavala.

Toilet paper

A delicate subject, but an important one. Due to the small bore of waste pipes that are used in Greece (no....I don't know why they don't use larger ones either), it is a rule that toilet paper is not flushed, but deposited in the bin by the toilet. Although this can be a little embarrassing for some, it is better than having to call on the manager of your accommodation to help unblock the toilet. However, the bins are emptied on a regular basis and shouldn't cause a problem.

Tipping

Tipping is an awkward subject to cover as it is obviously dependant on the quality of service you have received and at your personal discretion. The service you should receive on Thassos is usually very good and if you take an average price for a meal for two of 30 euro, a tip of 10 -15% is not excessive and quite acceptable, being about £2 - £3. The local wages are low and it may also be courteous (and prudent) to tip within these limits.

Hair dryers

Many of the higher quality hotels and apartments supply a hairdryer in the room. If this is an important accessory, check with your tour-company or hotel before leaving home.

Electric razors

Some accommodation on the island have dedicated razor points in the bathrooms, but if not the adaptors sold on the island will take a twin pin razor plug.

Police

There are police stations in nearly every large village or town. You will recognize the police station by the Greek flag flying from the building and of course by the police vehicles parked outside.

On Thassos during the summer, there is also a tourist police service (Touristiki Astinomia) for more holiday related problems. You will find the office of the tourist police in the same building as the island police in Thassos Town, directly on the harbour front.

The tourist police also supply information and brochures on the island and can help in searching for accommodation.

Tourist police office Thassos Town, tel: (25930) 23111

Post

As it is a tradition with us Brits to send home the usual 'wish you were here' cards, I will cover posting on the island, but remember even if you post your cards soon after your arrival, it is highly likely you will be home before your cards.

The cost of the postcards and the stamps required for the UK is very low and you can purchase both in the supermarkets.

The Greek postal service is ELTA and post offices can be found in all the larger towns and are usually open from 07:30 to 14:00. Post boxes are coloured bright yellow and the signs for a post-office are blue and yellow.

Fire prevention

In the summer months, the vegetation on the island becomes parched and tinder dry. In the past, the island has been ravaged by bush and forest fires and therefore it is essential to be careful, especially with discarded cigarettes. It is a law on the island that barbeques and campfires are banned outside the town areas so be warned!

Alexander the Great Airport

Sadly this information will only be of interest when you are returning home. The facilities are modern and as comfortable as any departure area. Once you pass through 'passport control', there are toilets, a café supplying drinks and snacks and a small duty-free shop selling the usual cigarettes, booze and a range of those last-minute present ideas.

Google Earth

For those with web access, an interesting and informative site is:-

www.earth.google.com

Here you can view satellite images of Thassos (and the whole world). You will need to download the free basic version software, but it is well worth it. For quick access to satellite images of Thassos, add the following coordinates into the top left-hand corner box and press search. This will take you to Thassos Town.

40 46 45.27N 24 42 34.10E

Concierge service

For those who want more than just the written word on Thassos as a guide, we offer a Concierge service that ranges from organising hotels, apartments, car hire and excursions, to personally escorting visitors around the island or the mainland, to introduce them to the wonders of the area.

The service is offered on an hourly or daily basis and the costs are dependant on the service requested. However, past experience has shown that with our help and knowledge, the amount you save, more than covers the Concierge charges.

If you would like that 'little extra', or a VIP service, please contact us on the email address below. We can then discuss your needs and confirm how we may be able to make your holiday even more memorable.

Our email is: info@a-to-z-guide.co.uk

Other services available include:-

Visiting the archaeological sites
'Special' days out
Champagne dinners
Shopping trips, male/female
Sports and activity booking
Property purchase/long term rental

Glossary of Greek words and phrases

Below, I have included a few useful words with their Greek counterparts. Although the majority of Greeks on the island speak some level of English (many putting us Brits to shame), I have found that they really appreciate our attempt to use their language, even if we make a proverbial 'pigs ear' of it.

Yes	Neh
No	Okhee
Good morning	Kalimera
Good afternoon/evening	Kalispaira
Please	Parakalo
Thank you	Efharisto
No, thank you	Okhee efharisto
The bill please	To logargiasmo parakalo, or simply make a gesture in the air as though you were signing your name.....it works!
Hello/Goodbye (singular/informal)	Yiassou
Hello/Goodbye (plural/formal)	Yassas
How much	Poso Kani
Coffee	Kafe
Tea	Tsai
OK	Endaksi

Where is	Pooh eeneh
Do you speak English	Meelahteh ahnggleekah
I don't understand	Dhehn kahtahlahvehno
Can I have	Boro nah ehkho
Can we have	Boroomeh nah ehkhoomeh
I'd like	Thah eethehlah
Tomorrow	Avrio
Today	Seemera
Toilets	To tooalettes
Wine	Krassi
Good	Kahloss
Bad	Kahkoss
Bank	Trapeza
Police	Astinomeea
Doctor	Yeeastros
Now	Toteh
What is the time	Ti ora ine
Cheers	Yammas
Sorry/excuse me	Signomee

Archaeological sites in Thassos Town

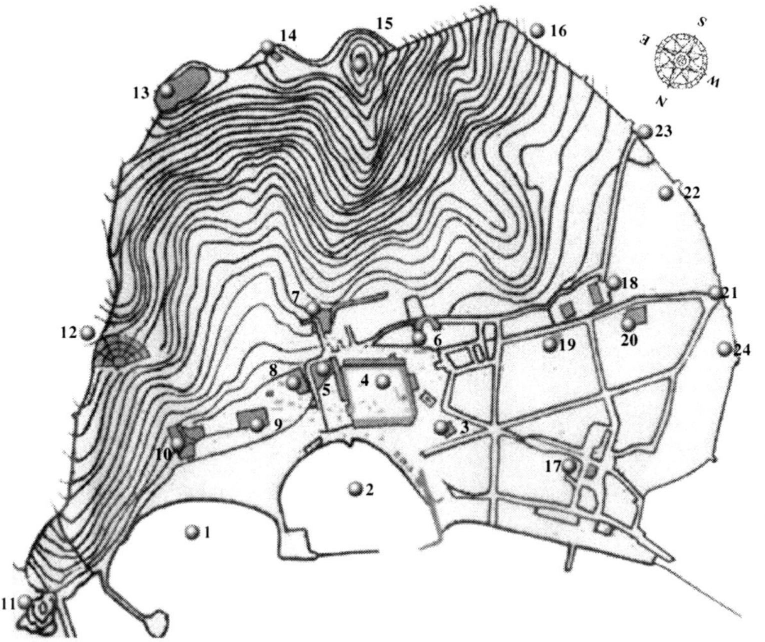

Group one

1. Ancient commercial harbour
2. Ancient fortified naval harbour
3. Archaeological museum
4. Agora
5. Roman quarters
6. Odeum
7. Artemision
8. Dionysion
9. Poseidonion and Gate of the Goddess on the Chariot
10. North quarter and Gate of Hermes and the three Graces
11. Evreocastro
12. Ancient theatre
13. Sanctuary of Apollo and Byzantine castle
14. Sanctuary of Athena
15. Sanctuary of Pan
16. Gate of Parmenon (off the beaten track and so I leave it to your discretion)

Group two

17. Early Christian Basilica
18. Heraclion
19. Arch of Caracalla
20. Necropolis artifacts
21. Gate of Zeus and Hera and sarcophagus of Poliades
22. Gate of Heracles and Dionysus
23. Gate of Silenus
24. Un-excavated gate (little to see)

Map of the Agora

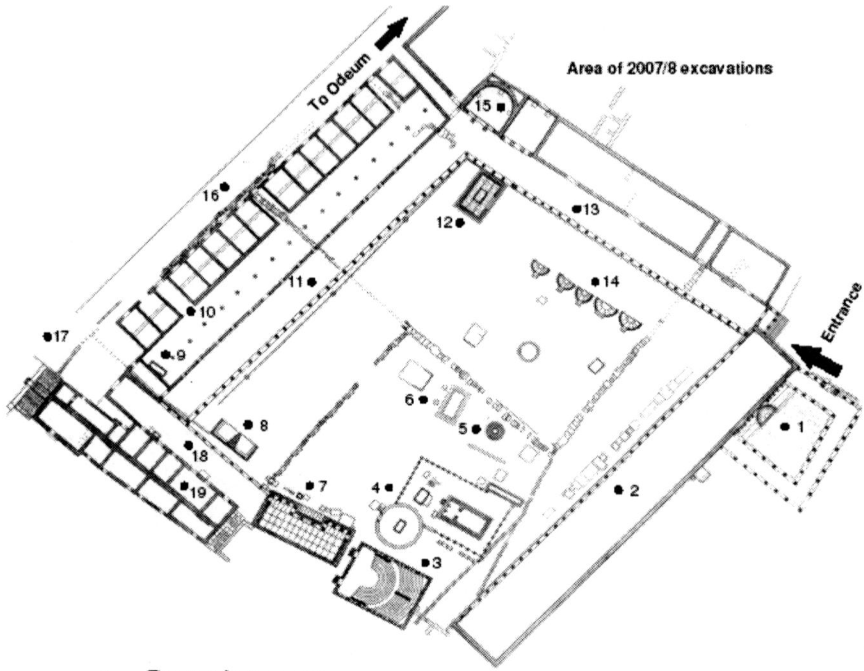

1. Roman law courts
2. Northwest stoa
3. Prytaneum
4. Sanctuary of Zeus Agoraios
5. Statue and altar to Theagenis
6. Altar to Gaius and Lucius Caesar, Augustus' grandsons
7. Greek law courts
8. Base of a statue to a naval victory
9. Tomb of Glaukos
10. Shops and workshops
11. Southeast stoa
12. Large altar
13. Southwest stoa
14. Row of exedrae
15. Apsidal room
16. Great Main Road
17. Passage of Theoroi
18. Short northeast stoa
19. Work and storerooms

Map of Philippi

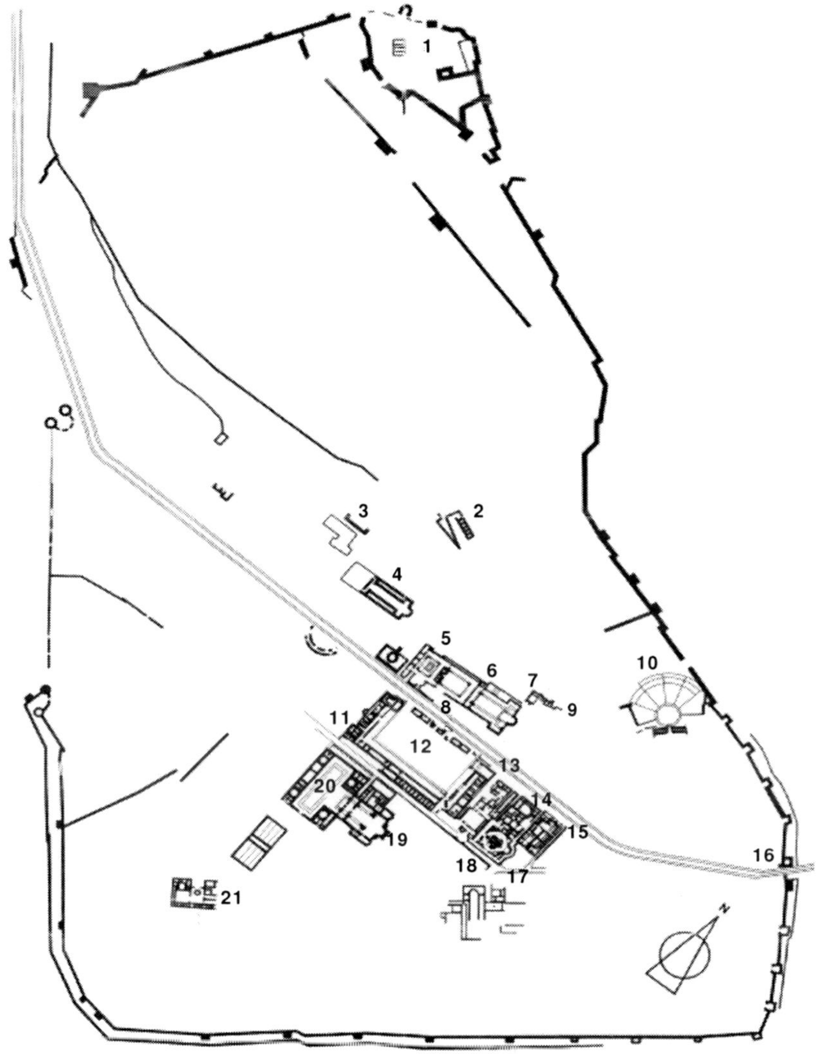

1. Acropolis
2. Sanctuary of the Egyptian gods
3. Museum
4. Basilica 'C'
5. Heroon
6. Basilica 'A'
7. Temple of the three niches
8. 'Prison' of St. Paul
9. Sanctuary of Silvanus
10. Ancient theatre
11. Commercial agora
12. Forum
13. Via Egnatia
14. Roman baths
15. Bishop's palace
16. Neapolis gate
17. Funerary heroon
18. Octagonal church
19. Basilica 'B'
20. Palaestra
21. Roman baths

Acknowledgements and web sites of interest:

I would like to thank the following for their help in the writing of this book.

Helene Katsorche, National Statistical Service of Greece
Konstantina Panousi, Archaeologist responsible for the island of Thassos
Yannis at Zorba's for his Greek food knowledge
The people of Thassos
Wikipedia
gWebsolutions

I have also included web pages on the island that you may find of interest.

www.gothassos.com

www.dnconsult.co.uk/thassos

www.gothassos.ws

www.go-thassos.gr

www.greekisland.co.uk/thassos/thassos.htm

www.thassosestate.com

http://www.greeka.com/eastern_aegean/thassos/index.htm

Notes

Printed in the United Kingdom
by Lightning Source UK Ltd.
134223UK00001B/185/P